Soft Furnishing Workshops

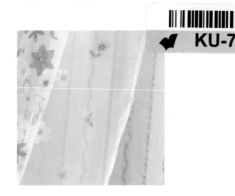

Curtains
and Blinds

Professional
skills made easy

hamlyn

Contents

First published in Great Britain
in 2001 by
Hamlyn, an imprint of Octopus
Publishing Group Ltd
2-4 Heron Quays, London E14 4JP

Copyright © Octopus Publishing
Group Ltd 1997, 2001

Distributed in the United States and
Canada by
Sterling Publishing Co., Inc.
387 Park Avenue South,
New York, NY 10016-8810

ISBN 0 600 60230 3

A CIP catalogue record for this book
is available from the British Library

Printed and bound in China

The Publishers have made every
effort to ensure that all instructions
given in this book are accurate and
safe, but they cannot accept liability
for any resulting injury, damage or
loss to either person or property
whether direct or consequential
and howsoever arising.

This book first appeared as part of
The Hamlyn Book of Soft Furnishings

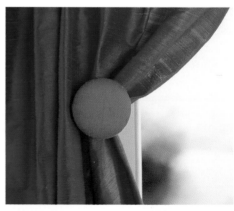

Metric and imperial measurements

Both metric and imperial measurements have been given in the instructions throughout this book. You should choose to work in either metric or imperial but, to ensure the success of your projects, do not mix the measurements.

Introduction

WINDOWS ARE SAID to be the eyes of a house. They give a room light and vitality, so it is important to make the most of the windows in your home. However, you need to get the right balance between various factors: allowing as much light to flood in as possible, dressing windows in a way that complements their style as well as that of the whole room, excluding draughts and gaining any necessary privacy.

It may sound demanding, but the secret is simply to take things slowly. Look in magazines and brochures for inspiration and start making a scrapbook of pictures that appeal to you.

Style

The details that make up a room's style include everything from the wall and floor finishes to the ornaments and flower arrangements. Fabrics and

soft furnishings need to be chosen to suit the overall design, and can make a major style statement in any room. Experiment with colour and furnishing schemes until you find the one that suits you and your lifestyle. Decide whether you want the room to appear bright or dark, cool or warm, then try out paint colours and large samples of wallpapers and furnishing fabrics to see how they all blend in together. By learning how to mix and match colours, patterns, textures and accessories and by following your design instincts, you will soon create an attractive scheme.

Left *An eclectic mix of styles and patterns suggests an oriental influence in this very individual-looking bedroom, with its minimalist lines, coordinated soft furnishings and striking rich colours.*

Above *Any room scheme that contains cream and off-white fabrics will be restful, calming, light and warm to live in. Sheer fabrics, such as muslin, filter rather than keep out bright sunlight*

Light and aspect
Major considerations as you begin to choose the fabrics for dressing windows for any house or room are location, aspect and the available light, which will affect the amount of sunshine and type of light that comes into the room.

Rooms in cool climates may be warmed up with dark fabrics, which absorb light and retain heat. Strong sunshine deadens colours and bleaches them, so special care must be taken in choosing

the type and colour of fabric. Silk, for example, is prone to fail in bright sunlight; blues and reds are more susceptible to fading than other colours, and natural dyes will fade faster than modern chemical dyes. These potential problems can be avoided by adding some good-quality linings to curtains.

Whereas country rooms normally face outward to take best advantage of the surroundings, city rooms often need to look inward. Their window treatments therefore become important focal points and need to be as attractive as they are

functional. Roman blinds can show fabric to its best advantage and can look as smart when fully raised in concertina pleats as they do when fully lowered. They also give you full control of the light and the apartment's outlook.

Choosing fabric

There are endless fabric patterns and textures from which you can choose, and only you can decide on the style and colour combinations that appeal to you – be it beautiful voiles or muslin (which in generous amounts, can create romantic, billowing curtains), the soft spring colours of a floral print coordinated with a striped fabric, a rich print with geometric blocks of colour, discreet neutrals or vibrant plain colours in more formal fabrics such as wool and silk. Very often, a pattern can be the starting point for a complete colour scheme, the colours in the pattern providing the basic colour palette for paints, plain fabrics and other accessories.

It is very difficult choosing fabric from a small swatch – a plain colour can take on different hues in a large piece, and large patterns are completely

Above *Rich silk taffeta looks best draped and tied, so that the light catches on the folds.*

Right *Blue and white are perennial favourites. Crisp stripes and simple gingham checks, joined by prints and other tones of blue, work equally well in kitchen, country sitting room or bedroom schemes.*

lost on small fabric clippings. If you cannot obtain large samples, buy at least 0.5m (¹/₂yd) of any selected materials to check at home. No colour will be the same in all lights – or even in different parts of the same room – so do not expect to get an exact match.

Always check curtaining fabrics with the light behind the material, not in front – unless you have windows on opposite or adjacent walls, the light will always be behind the fabric. Most woven cloths need light thrown on them to bring out their pattern. Hang and drape your samples where they will be used, and look at them through the day. They might look quite different in the morning and afternoon, and artificial light can bring further changes.

Influences and imagination

If you are looking for a starting point for a style to suit your home, step back and think about the particular interests and passions in your life, so that you can build up a style around a theme. If you love gardening for example, a floral theme or leafy green colours can set the style of a room. If you enjoy travel, you can have fun planning your room schemes around different countries – think about developing a richly coloured Indian living room or a sunny French kitchen. Alternatively, build a room scheme around a favourite collection of antiques or ornaments, choosing paints, wallpapers and fabrics to blend in with the collection's colours. The options are limited only by your imagination.

The evolution of curtains

Window curtains, as we know them, have been around only about 300 years. In medieval times heavy tapestries were used to cover doorways, to partition off parts of rooms for privacy, and to hang all the way around beds to keep out draughts. Windows at this time, however, were always left bare. It was not until well into the 16th century that window curtains, made of one piece of

Top *Take in all the details around you when away from home. Painted walls, wooden shutters and colourful canopies may all suggest a previously unimagined decorative scheme for your home.*

Above *Nature is valuable inspiration for the perfect colour scheme.*

material suspended from an iron rod, with rings or ties to hold them in place, started to appear.

By the late 17th century, window curtains had started to become an essential part of a room's decorative scheme. The single curtain had already been divided into two – its arrangement in pairs part of a more symmetrical approach to interiors – but now elaborate pelmets and draperies were constructed to hide fittings. In wealthy homes, soft, ruched valances began to appear at the tops of windows and even pull-up curtains started to be seen. In modest homes, curtains were made of dark wool cloth.

Roller and Venetian blinds began to be used in the 18th century. The 19th century saw windows

Above *Today's simple approach to dressing windows is a far cry from the cluttered window treatments so popular with the Victorians.*

dressed in layers: heavy drapery thrown over ornamental poles to form a swag-style pelmet (later replaced by the lambrequin), and combined with silk or wool curtains, behind which were lace or muslin under-curtains and a blind. Towards the end of the 19th century the cluttered window treatments began to give way to the simpler approaches known today. Today's curtains are still inspired by past styles to some extent, but have been toned down to suit our more modest homes.

Ideas and projects

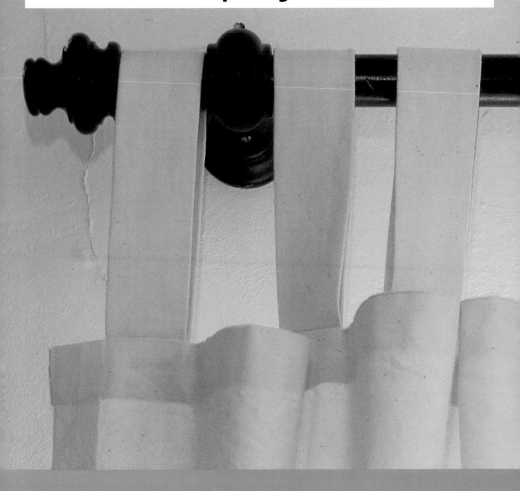

CURTAINS AND BLINDS come in such a huge variety of styles and fabrics, that when you are choosing a window treatment for a room, the problem is often that there is too much choice rather than too little. What is most important is to find the look that fits best into your room, whether the setting is modern or traditional, and that suits your needs in practical terms, too.

Whether you prefer formal dressings, simple unlined curtains, the layered look or flat-faced blinds that show off boldly designed fabric, there are plenty of ideas and projects on the following pages to inspire you and encourage you to make your own customized curtains or blinds for your home.

Window dressing

WINDOW TREATMENTS should always be devised as part of the overall scheme of a room. This means looking at the colours, the style, the patterns and period of the room and its decor, and means choosing fabrics and a treatment that work well in that setting. However attractive you may think a certain fabric appears in the shop, or however appealing a window treatment looks in a magazine, if it does not relate to the rest of your room, the results will be disappointing. For inspiration, you could also take a look at some of the coordinated ranges of fabrics that allow you to make blinds, pelmets, tie-backs, voile drapes and other accessories in colours and patterns to match your chosen curtain fabric.

New room schemes

If you are starting from scratch with your room scheme, you have much more freedom and leeway in choosing your decor. If you choose a multi-coloured curtaining fabric for example, you can pick out the colour of the wallpaper and paint colours from it. Mix-while-you-wait paint ranges allow you to find an almost perfect colour match.

The details of your window treatment also need careful consideration. Do you want tie-backs, or to edge the curtains with braid or a contrasting trimming? Would you like to add rosettes, on tie-backs for example ? Browse through magazines for inspiration, and look around you for ideas you visit hotels, restaurants and other people's homes.

Choosing fabrics

When you find a fabric that you like, ask if you can borrow a large swatch from the store to try out in the actual room – many retailers are prepared to lend fabric on payment of a deposit. Or consider buying a short length of the fabric. Light – especially artificial light – can play tricks on fabrics and the way it looks in the shop is

Right *Coordinating ranges of fabrics and wallpapers make for easy colour scheming. A deep, shaped lambrequin adds importance to lined curtains in this bedroom.*

unlikely to be the way it will appear in your home.

Always take plenty of time when you are choosing fabric. Do not try to rush the process. The money and time invested in creating window treatments can be considerable so it is really important to be sure that you are going to be happy with the results. Fabric usually needs to be used generously for the best effect, so it is important that you are sure that you have chosen the right materials before you spend your money.

Window shape

Some windows need only a very simple approach to display them at their best, especially if

Above right *The warm yellow colour of the draped curtain fabric and the simple style of the window treatment have been carefully chosen to complement the character and decor of this room. The narrow ribbon tied around the curtain fabric complements the blue and white accessories.*

Right *Blinds are particularly suited for bold designs since, when lowered, the fabric lies flat. This bathroom has been carefully coordinated throughout – the birds on the blind continue the seashore theme of the shells around the bath.*

they are particularly attractive. Unusual window designs or shapes, such as arched or pointed Gothic windows or pretty leaded cottage casements, need only restrained window dressing in order to show them off to their best effect.

Café curtains, which cover only the lower part of the window, are a good choice for windows with an interesting shape at the top. They are also ideal where you need some privacy, such as at a kitchen window that overlooks a street. Voile works well with unusual window shapes, too, as it can be fitted around the actual arch itself with special touch-and-close curtain tape. (At night anyone outside will be able to see in when you have a light on, so this treatment will work only in the right situation.)

Above right *Since this circular window is a stunning feature in its own right, any attempt to cover it with curtains or blinds would be a mistake. The sill is a perfect home for personal collections such as these shells.*

Right *Blinds like this roller blind are the ideal option for windows where there is no space on either side to draw back curtains, or for recessed windows that need to be screened but not insulated.*

Blinds

Blinds are good for an uncluttered look, since most lift up out of the way to leave the window clear. Windows where there is no space on either side to draw the curtain back into, such as dormer windows or windows that fully occupy alcoves, are also a perfect candidate for blinds. Roman and roller blinds are not difficult to make at home and have the added advantage of being very economical with fabric.

Bare windows

Some windows do not need any coverage at all. If privacy is not an issue and you have a particularly interesting window, then leave it bare. Windows with stained glass are also best left uncovered so as to be displayed to best effect. Not only are they attractive but they can be particularly useful for awkward-to-reach areas, such as high up in stairwells, where daily curtain pulling or blind lowering would be difficult.

Light

The natural light in a room is another important factor when you choose a window treatment. If the room is airy with plenty of natural light, allowing the sunshine to stream in through voiles and unlined cotton can be very effective. On the other hand, the same room could be given a more formal treatment and not lose out on too much light even if the drapes partially obscure the windows.

If a room is badly lit, because of trees or a wall outside the window or because it faces north, then you should ideally use a pale-coloured fabric arranged in such a way that it does not block out too much light. You can also pick a colour scheme for the whole room that reflects as much light into the room as possible.

Above *Voile hung from a pole above an unusual window, like this attractive arch, allows the shape of the window to be seen through the fabric.*

Making decisions and measuring up

BEFORE YOU CAN START to make your curtains, you need to buy the fabric, and in order to work out how much to buy, you must have your curtain pole or track in position and you need to measure up. You will need to make some decisions – as long as you work logically through the whole process, you will find all the details soon fall into place.

Decisions to make

There is so much choice today with window treatments that it can be very difficult to know where to start. Work through the following checklist first to determine your particular requirements and help you decide what you want.

- Do you want to hide a view, or is a particular window overlooked? Try using sheers and blinds; a multi-layered look will give flexibility.

- Do you want to make the most of a lovely outlook? If so, keep the treatment simple, especially if privacy is not a consideration, and ensure you can draw curtains well back from the window.

- Will you need to open and close the curtains or blinds frequently? This can be particularly troublesome

Curtain length

- Curtains can hang to the sill, a little below the sill, or to the floor.

- For a more formal treatment or a larger room, opt for floor-length curtains.

- Sill-length curtains or just below sill-length curtains are best for small rooms such as guest bedrooms, kitchens and bathrooms.

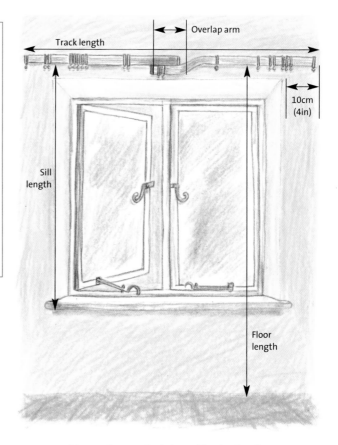

Above *Casement window with a track system.*

with inward-opening casement windows. So choose corded track or a very simple treatment.

- Is it important to keep light out or to keep heat in? Heavier fabric and thermal or blackout lining, or even interlining are good in this situation.

- Are the proportions of the window satisfactory or do you want to disguise them in some way? This can be surprisingly simple to do with the right treatment (see page 22).

Measuring up

Measuring up is probably the most important part of curtain-making. It sounds complicated but if you follow the steps below methodically it is quite simple. Use a calculator for speed and accuracy.

- THE FINISHED WIDTH
  To find out what the finished width of the curtains should be, measure from one end of the track or pole (excluding finials) to the other (see illustrations below). If you have a track with an overlap arm you need to measure that too and add it to the measurement.

- OVERALL FABRIC WIDTH
  Decide on how full your curtains need to be; even when drawn, they should still appear gathered. Choose your heading (see pages 24–27) as this will affect the fullness of the curtains. You then need to multiply your finished width by the amount required for fullness. This will give you your overall fabric width.

- THE NUMBER OF WIDTHS
  To get fabric panels for wide windows you may need to join fabric widths. Divide the overall fabric width required by the width of the fabric as it is sold. Round this figure up or down to the nearest whole number. This will give you the number of widths that you need. If the total comes to an odd number and you are having two curtains, you need to cut one width in half lengthways and sew one piece on to each curtain.

Pole length

10cm (4in)

Sill length

Floor length

Above *Sash window with a traditional curtain pole.*

- OVERALL FABRIC DROP
  Decide how long you want
  your curtains to be. Measure
  from the bottom of the track
  or curtain rings to where
  you want the bottom of the
  finished curtains to come.
  You need to do this in several
  places to check whether your
  window and floor are even.
  Add to this measurement
  about 23cm (9in) for turnings
  and hems at the top and
  bottom (the exact amount
  will depend on the curtains
  you are making, so do
  remember to check all the
  instructions first. This figure
  is your overall fabric drop
  measurement.

- TOTAL FABRIC REQUIREMENT
  When you have arrived at
  your overall fabric drop
  measurement, multiply this
  by the number of widths
  that are needed. This final
  amount will then give you
  the total fabric required for
  your curtain project.

- ALLOWING FOR PATTERNS
  With patterned fabrics you
  have to match the design

Right *Cottage windows,
especially with deep reveals like
this one, can be tricky to dress. As
with dormer windows, curtains
can be unsuccessful here as they
cannot be drawn away from the
window on either side. A simple
blind would be a good choice
here.*

when joining widths. Add the pattern repeat size (it may be printed on the selvage or else ask the manufacturer) on to each width or your fabric drop measurement. If the pattern is half drop you will have to add one and a half times this measurement to the overall fabric drop measurement. Position bold motifs at the bottom of a curtain, so that you do not cut off any pattern (see far left). Always check that the pattern matches across all widths before cutting out (see left).

Summary of calculations

Set out your calculations as follows:

- Length of track or pole + any overlap = finished curtain width

- Finished curtain width × fullness = overall fabric width

- Overall fabric width ÷ width of chosen fabric = number of widths

- Fabric drop measurement + allowance for turnings + any extra for pattern repeats = overall fabric drop measurement

- Overall fabric drop measurement × number of widths = total fabric amount

NOTE: work in either inches or centimetres . Divide the total fabric amount by 100 to give the number of metres if you are working in centimetres, or by 36 to give the number of yards if you are working in inches.

Left *To work out the length of fabric required for unusual window treatments like this one, experiment with a length of spare fabric or by looping a tape measure in the required style.*

Tracks and poles

TRACKS AND CURTAIN POLES can play a very important part in the overall look of window treatments, so you need to put almost as much time into choosing an appropriate one as you do your fabric. There are many decorative poles available, and some very inspiring designs – in cast iron, wood and brass. Curtain poles usually have decorative ends called finials. These come in a stunning range of shapes and materials. Examples include metal ones shaped like arrowheads, wooden ones carved like pineapples and even frosted glass spirals in acid colours. So if you do opt for this sort of decorative pole, make sure that it fits with your room style and curtains.

But whereas you might choose a pole so that it can be seen, curtain track is usually chosen to be as discreet as possible. With some designs, the track is completely hidden by the curtains when they are drawn. Others consist of very plain track with the curtains hanging below. Sometimes it is possible to stick wallpaper or paint on to the track's surface to camouflage it. Alternatively, you could conceal the track with a valance or pelmet.

Choosing tracks

Some tracks come ready-corded, so that you never need to touch the curtains but can open and close them by pulling a cord at one side. Cord tensioners, which keep the cord tidy and out of the way, are available. Automatic systems are also available: these allow you to set times for the curtains to open and close, which can be very useful if you are away from home a lot.

With a track system you can have an overlap in the middle of the curtains. You can also buy multi-layer track, which allows you to hang sheer curtains and a valance from the same brackets. You can also buy tracks that are disguised behind false pole fronts. These do offer some of the advantages of a track system, but tend to be limited to just a few traditional styles.

Weight considerations

You also need to think about how strong you need your pole or track to be, especially if you wish to hang heavy drapes. Poles vary in thickness and metal tracks tend to be stronger than

Above *Decorative finials come in a whole host of shapes and materials. Many styles offer hold-backs to match.*

Right *The size of the finial needs to be in proportion with the pole.*

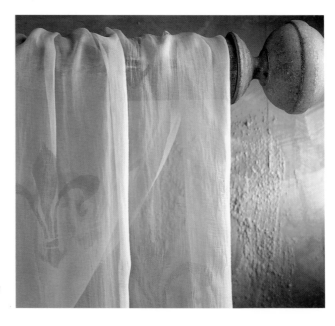

Right *Tracks and poles now come in an enormous range of metals, woods and plastics, and are available in many different shapes and sizes, so you are bound to find one to complement your chosen window treatment. Make sure that your track or pole also suits your practical needs and is suitable for fixing to your walls.*

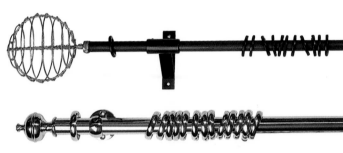

Left *Poles can be a stunning feature in their own right. Here, a shapely hand-forged metal pole is given a red and gold tassel as a stunning finishing touch.*

plastic ones. Manufacturers usually state on the packaging the weight that their products will hold. Obviously, tracks and poles are only as strong as their fixings, so also make sure that they are firmly fitted in place and regularly supported along their length (see pages 70–72).

Awkward windows

If you have bay windows in your home the easiest choice is track as there are products that you can bend around corners and curves. Make sure the track is designed for this before you buy – not all track is suitable. If you prefer to have poles, you can buy adjustable corner fittings that allow you to link wooden poles. Some companies will make you iron poles to order, but be sure

Above right *Some tracks and poles can be adapted to fit around bay windows. Poles can be made to measure or they can be fitted with adjustable corner brackets, while some curtain tracks are designed so that they can be bent around corners.*

Disguising oddly shaped windows

If your windows are not quite the shape you would like there is a lot you can do to alter the visual effect.

- Short windows will look taller if you fix the curtain track or pole much higher than usual above the window and have curtains that reach down to the floor.

- Tall windows will look shorter if you position the track or pole as low as possible and add a deep fabric pelmet or valance.

- Wide windows look narrower if the track or pole is as short as possible and the curtains are permanently joined at the top and draped open with hold-backs or tie-backs.

- Narrow windows will appear wider if the track or pole extends well to either side of the window and is hung with generous, full-length curtains.

to measure up accurately. If someone from the company will measure up for you then you are covered if the pole does not fit.

Sizing up

Before you buy your pole or track, consider its length, as this will govern the width of curtains that you should make. Poles and tracks need to extend beyond the window on either side to allow the curtains to be drawn out of the way, otherwise they will obscure the view and cut out light.

Below *Visually striking poles and finials are shown to their best advantage when used with fairly plain, simply draped fabric.*

Headings and tapes

AFTER CHOOSING THE WIDTH of your curtain track or pole, you also need to decide on the fullness of your curtains before you can calculate the fabric needed. Even when they are drawn, with most curtain styles the fabric should still look full rather than flat. This fullness is achieved by sewing special tape on to the top of the back of the curtains and drawing up the pull-cords to gather the fabric into pleats. Alternatively, curtains can be gathered without tape, by folding and sewing the pleats into place by hand. This is more time consuming but can give a very classy, tailored effect (see pages 40–42).

Buying headings and tapes

Curtain tapes come in many varieties, giving all sorts of effects. The simplest of all is standard curtain tape, which is 2.5cm (1in) deep and gives a straightforward gathered effect. Pencil pleats are deeper and more regular, and are usually about 7.5cm (3in) deep. Fancier headings such as triple pleats, goblet pleats and lattice pleats

Below *Pencil-pleat headings call for generous amounts of fabric and are particularly suited for floor-length curtains.*

require even deeper headings.
These different headings give
varying amounts of fullness to
the curtains, ranging from half
as full again as ungathered
fabric for standard tape to three
times as full for some pencil-
pleat headings.

Curtains should look
generous but not too full. Take
into account the fabric you are

choosing: heavy fabric does not
need to be as full as finer fabric
in order to look good. Similarly,
lined (and especially interlined)
curtains, too, do not need to be
as full as their unlined
counterparts. Very occasionally,
however, you may want curtains
to be ungathered. Informal
effects where fabric is tied on
to a curtain pole with lengths of

Above *Curtains can be fitted
directly on to pelmet box shelves
with self-adhesive touch-and-
close fastening and special
curtain tape.*

Heading tapes

Front   *Back*

Simple gathered heading

Triple-pinch pleating

Pencil pleating

Box pleating

Goblet pleating

Detachable lining tape

ribbon or with fabric ties and bunched up with casual folds can look good in certain settings, or you may wish to hang flat panels of lace or fabric over glazed doors or small windows.

Choosing fabric

- Never skimp on curtain fabric. Tight curtains look mean, however attractive the fabric. Just choose something less expensive and buy more fabric.

- Always buy the best-quality fabric you can afford.

- You normally make curtains as part of a room scheme so choose the design and colour to suit the other furnishings. Take paint, carpet, wallpaper and other samples with you when you go shopping.

- Ask the store if you can borrow a large sample of fabric to take home with you.

Right *The pinch-pleat heading is simple yet elegant for these semi-formal curtains. The track has been disguised by a strip of matching fabric. A coordinating Roman blind and a sheer complete the treatment.*

- Fabrics with large patterns can be very wasteful of fabric as you have to buy extra to match up the repeats (see pages 18–19). Matching up repeats can also be difficult, so avoid large patterns if you are on a tight budget or if you are new to curtain-making.

- Check that the fabric will drape nicely. There is little you can do to make stiff fabric drape well, but you can add extra body to lighter-weight fabric by lining or even interlining it.

Draw-cord tidy

Do not cut the draw-cords after gathering, or you will not be able to flatten the curtain for cleaning. Instead, make a small bag to hold them neatly.

Cut a rectangle of lining fabric 9 × 21cm (3½ × 8¼in). Turn under the bottom edge to the wrong side to form a narrow hem, and stitch. Fold up the lower section of the strip, right sides together, so that the neatened edge is 3cm (1¼in) below the top raw edge. Stitch up the two sides, trim the corners and seams. Turn right way out and press, ironing the side raw edges under at the same time.

While sewing the heading tape in place, catch in the top part of the bag along the tape's lower edge. Secure the cords and store them in the bag.

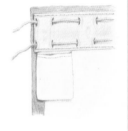

Left *A cased heading requires no tapes and curtain rings or any complicated sewing. Two parallel rows of stitching along the top edge create a slot through which a curtain pole can be slipped. This door curtain is held out of the way with two tasselled tie-backs.*

Hold-backs

HOLD-BACKS AND TIE-BACKS have become popular because they give an attractive, stylish line to curtains when they are drawn back. Hold-backs are rigid and usually made from wood or metal. They can be in the form of a disc or a decorative shape on the end of a short rod, over which the curtain is draped; some are like very large hooks behind which the curtain is tucked.

If you have chosen a pole with decorative finials for your curtain you may be able to buy matching hold-backs. Otherwise, look for designs that complement your room's style. Some hold-backs are quite formal, while others have more novelty value.

If you cannot find a curtain hold-back that you particularly like, you can easily cover a plain, circular wooden one yourself with fabric. The hold-back might get a bit 'lost' if you covered it with the same fabric as your curtain, so try using a coordinating or a contrasting fabric instead.

Above *A hold-back is an elegant way of drawing back curtains during the day, particularly if you have chosen a traditional or rather dramatic window treatment. This large brass hold-back is the perfect complement for the room's luxurious drapes and richly coloured walls.*

Covering a wooden hold-back

PREPARING THE FABRIC

Measure the diameter of the hold-back disc and double it. Cut out a circle this diameter from paper or thin card and use it as a template to cut out fabric for each of the hold-backs. Neaten the raw edges of the circles either by overlocking or making a small turning. Then run a strong gathering thread near the edge of the circle.

If you would like a slightly more padded look to your hold-back, cut a circle of wadding about 4cm (1½in) smaller in diameter than your fabric circle and centre it on the wrong side of the fabric. Baste close to the edge of the wadding.

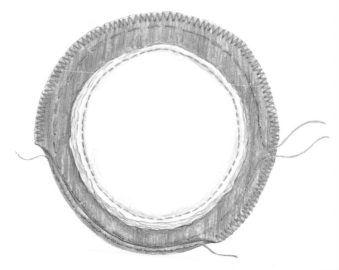

COVERING THE HOLD-BACK

Place the fabric over the hold-back and pull up the gathering thread to fit around the rod at the back and fasten off the ends of the thread securely. Wind seam binding around the back to hold the gathers in place, adding a few stitches to hold the binding, if preferred.

You could add a motif to the front, such as a starfish or a carved wooden shape, if liked. Secure it in place with strong adhesive such as epoxy resin.

Left *For a modern look a simple hold-back can be covered in bright fabric that contrasts with your curtain, such as this vibrant blue and pink colour combination.*

Tie-backs

LIKE HOLD-BACKS, curtain tie-backs are practical as well as decorative. They allow you to pull the curtains back from the window to gain the maximum amount of daylight. They may take the form of corded tassels that loop around the curtains, or can be made of fabric to match the curtains. Tie-backs are usually fixed on to hooks on the wall close to the edge of the window. Some tie-back hooks can be a little utilitarian: ornate ones are available from curtain accessory manufacturers. The positioning of the tie-back on the window depends on the effect that you want.

Above *Tie-backs are useful at either end of wide windows, or for curtains across bay or bow windows. They hold the bulk of the fabric out of the way during the day. Check how bulky the curtains are when drawn back and make the tie-back short enough to pull them in and drape attractively.*

Left *Positioning the tie-back as high as possible, particularly if there is only a single curtain, allows maximum light through a window.*

Right *A fabric tie-back is simple to make, either in a matching fabric or one that coordinates with your curtains. As here, a lined, semicircular tail can be hung from the tie-back hook for extra detail, if preferred.*

Making fabric tie-backs

Fabric tie-backs are simple to make. This tie-back style is in the traditional crescent shape and has optional piping.

MEASURING AND CUTTING OUT

Measure around the drawn-back curtain with a tape measure and add 5cm (2in) to the measurement. Take a piece of thin card and cut a rectangle to the length of the measurement you have just taken, with a depth of 10–15cm (4–6in). Fold the length of card in half; using scissors, trim the edges to curve them slightly, then unfold the card. Check the

effect and adjust if necessary. From this template, cut one shape from iron-on interfacing for each tie-back. Add a 1.5cm (⅝in) seam allowance all round the pattern and use it to cut two fabric pieces for each tie-back.

ADDING INTERFACING AND PIPING

Centre the interfacing, adhesive side down, on the wrong side of one piece of fabric and press in place (see page 68). To pipe the tie-backs, make up a length of covered piping for each (see page 67) then pin and baste it around the seam allowance with raw edges matching. Snip the seam allowances to make the piping lie flat around the curves.

FINISHING THE TIE-BACK

Pin, then baste the remaining fabric piece on to each tie-back, right sides together. Machine stitch close to the piping, leaving a gap for turning the fabric the right side out. Trim and clip the seams, turn the right side out then press and slipstitch the opening. To make a 'tail', line two semicircles of fabric and attach one to the outer edge of each tie-back. Stitch a curtain ring on the back of each tie-back by which to hang it on the hook on the wall.

Unlined curtains

UNLINED CURTAINS have less body than lined curtains, so they do not hang as well, but they are easier to make and wash or clean, making them particularly ideal for use in kitchens, bathrooms and children's rooms. If you find that they let in too much light or you want to protect them from fading, you can always add a pair of detachable linings (see page 34).

Making unlined curtains

SUGGESTED FABRICS

Chintz, colour-woven cotton, gingham, floral prints

MATERIALS

Curtain fabric

Pencil-pleat tape – the length of the curtain fabric width plus 20cm (8in) for turnings

Curtain hooks to suit the tape

Scissors and sewing equipment

Matching sewing thread

MEASURING AND CUTTING OUT

Measure the window and calculate the fabric needed (see pages 16–19) – this heading needs 2½ times the width; add 16cm (6¼in) to each length for turnings. If joining fabric in an unlined curtain, use 1.5cm (⅝in) flat fell seams (see page 65).

FINISHING THE EDGES

Turn in the long side edges of the curtain lengths 1cm (⅜in) to the wrong side, then turn 1.5cm (⅝in) again and machine stitch in place down the length of the curtain.

Above *While some people prefer their bedroom to be as dark as possible, others like to be woken up by sunlight streaming in through the window. If the latter is your choice, then unlined curtains are your best option.*

MAKING THE HEM

Press under the bottom edge 7.5cm (3in) to the wrong side, then press another 7.5cm (3in) to form a double hem. Press. To mitre the corners, unfold the hem once and fold in the corner at an angle, from where the last hem meets the side edge to a point 1cm (³⁄₈in) in along the bottom edge. Press in place and then fold the hem back again. Overstitch the mitre, and hand stitch the hem neatly in place.

NEATENING THE TOP EDGE

Turn under a 6mm (¼in) single hem to the wrong side along the top edge. Press, pin and baste in place.

PREPARING THE TAPE

Cut a piece of pencil-pleat tape 10cm (4in) longer than the width of each finished curtain. At the end of each piece of tape that will be at the centre of the window, pull a 4cm (1½in) piece of each cord through to the back and knot. Trim the tape to 1.5cm (⁵⁄₈in) beyond the knot and press this end to the wrong side.

POSITIONING THE TAPE

Ensure the tape is the correct way up then position the knotted ends of the tape at the centre edges of the curtains with the tape's top edge 3mm (¹⁄₈in) below the top of the curtain. Pin in place. At the outer edges of each curtain pull the cords through to the front of the tape and trim the tape to 1.5cm (⁵⁄₈in) beyond the curtain edge; tuck under. Baste the tape in place then machine stitch along both edges, avoiding the cords. Stitch both rows in the same direction. Machine stitch across both turned-under short ends of the tape, leaving the cords free.

FINISHING THE CURTAIN

Draw up the cords from the outer edges of the curtain, pleating the fabric evenly until the curtain is the right width. Tie both of the cords together and then tuck them into a cord bag (see page 27), or alternatively wind them around a cord tidy. To finish, insert hooks in the tape about every 7.5cm (3in) and hang the curtains on a pole or track.

Slip hemming

Slip hemming, or blind hemming, employs stitches that are barely visible from either side of the fabric. Work from right to left, or towards you, with the lower edge of the hem away from you.

Bring the needle up through the fabric fold, then take a tiny stitch in the main fabric, picking up only one or two threads as you do so. Angle the needle diagonally and bring it up through the fabric's fold, about 6mm (¼in) along the hemline. Take a tiny stitch in the fold, then take the needle down and back through the main fabric, as before.

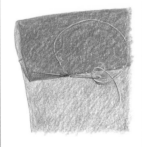

Making a pair of detachable linings

Detachable linings are simple to make, and can be made after the curtains they are to line. You need only 1½ times the pole or track width, so they are economical on fabric. Choose from ordinary, thermal or blackout lining.

MEASURING UP
The quantity of fabric needed depends whether you hang the lining on the same hooks as the curtains, or use special combined hooks and gliders. If you use the same hooks as the curtain, each length of lining fabric needs to be 7.5cm (3in) longer than the curtains. With combined hooks and gliders, the lengths of lining fabric need to be 5cm (2in) longer than the curtains.

MAKING THE HEMS
Turn under the hem allowances around the sides and across the lower edge, as for unlined curtains (see previous page). Cut lining tape for each curtain, each length to be 10cm (4in) longer than the fabric widths. Knot the cords at the centre edge of each tape (see previous page). Pin the lining tape on to the top of the linings, with the raw edge of the lining fabric between the 'skirts' of the tape and the knotted ends at the centre edges of each lining, with the tape extending 1cm (3/8in) beyond the centre edge. Check that the lining will

not hang down below the curtain's hem and adjust the length at the top, if necessary.

POSITIONING THE TAPE
Baste the tape in place, ensuring that you catch the back skirt of the tape. Turn the centre tape overhangs to the wrong side to form a double 5mm (3/16in) hem, to conceal the knots; baste in place. On the outer edges pull the cords free to the front of the tape, for about 5cm (2in). Trim the tape to form 1cm (3/8in)

overhangs, neaten as for the centre tape ends, but without catching the ends, then baste in place. Machine stitch along the bottom of the tape close to the edge, catching in the other side of the skirt, then machine stitch down the short ends, leaving the cords free. Remove the basting.

HANGING THE LININGS
Gather the linings. If your track has combined gliders and hooks insert the hooks so the lining will hang the right way round.

Left *This valance-style fixed curtain makes a small window look interesting. Since it is decorative it needs no lining.*

Above *Rustic-style windows need only a simple treatment; these unlined curtains hanging from a bamboo pole are ideal.*

Tie-on and tab-top curtains

CURTAINS WITH A BOUND EDGE in a contrasting colour look stylish but informal, and are easy to make. They are also easily lined, as here, by working with two thicknesses of fabric instead of one. You can choose a coordinating fabric for the lining, but not one that is so strongly patterned or coloured that it will show through to the front. Also use coordinating fabric for the ties, but make sure that all the fabrics used are of a similar weight and content.

Bound-edge curtains with ties

SUGGESTED FABRICS

Plain, printed or colour-woven cotton. Avoid bold designs or heavy fabrics

MATERIALS

Curtain fabric

Lining fabric (optional – same quantity as curtain fabric)

Coordinating fabric for binding and ties

Medium-weight iron-on interfacing – sufficient to cut strips 5cm (2in) deep by the total width of the curtains (you will need to butt up strips to join them)

Scissors and sewing equipment

Matching sewing thread

Curtain pole

MEASURING UP

Measure up from the curtain pole to the desired finished curtain length to determine fabric quantities required (see pages 16–19). You do not need to allow for hems or side turnings, unless joining fabric widths. You may have to allow extra for facings if your curtains are unlined. The lining should be the same size as the curtain.

Right *A coordinating plain bound edge gives these patterned drapes a stylish finish. These curtain ties are threaded through curtain rings, but could just as easily be tied directly around the curtain pole.*

CUTTING OUT

Cut the curtain fabric and lining fabric, if using, to size. To join fabric widths, use 1.5cm (⅝in) flat seams if the curtains will be lined, and press them open. If the curtains will be unlined, use flat fell seams (see page 65). Cut four pieces of binding, 6.5cm (2½in) wide, for each curtain: two pieces the length of the curtain, and two pieces the same as the width plus 3cm (1¼in). Work out how many ties you need to position them every 20cm (8in) across the curtain's width. Make up the required number of ties (see box below), 46cm (18in) long, from strips of fabric, 6.5cm (2½in) wide.

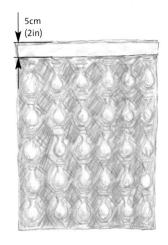

5cm
(2in)

APPLYING THE INTERFACING

Lay the curtain fabric face down and iron on strips of interfacing along the top (see page 68), following the manufacturer's instructions. Butt up the strips to join them where necessary.

POSITIONING THE LINING

Lay the lining on top of the curtain , with wrong sides facing and all raw edges level. Pin, then baste close to the edges. Turn the panel over so the right side of the curtain is uppermost.

BINDING THE EDGES

Press all of the binding pieces of fabric in half lengthways, with the wrong sides facing. Open them up, then press the raw edges in to meet the centre line. Pin the long binding strips along the long raw edges of the curtain fabric, with right sides facing and the raw edges level at the sides, top and bottom. Machine stitch along the first fold in the binding – 1.5cm (⅝in) in from the edge. Fold the

Making ties

Cut strips of fabric according to the number of ties required and to the pattern measurements. Fold each strip in half lengthways, right sides facing, and run some tape or cord along the length, close to the fold. Stitch across one end, catching the end of the tape or cord into the seam. Then stitch

along the long edge of each tie, taking a 1.5cm (⅝in) seam allowance, taking care not to catch the tape or cord in the seam. Trim the seam allowance of each tie and pull the tape or cord to turn it the right side out. Trim away the tape or cord, press each tie, then turn in the raw edges and slipstitch the opening.

binding around the seam allowance to the back of the curtain, tuck in the pressed fold and slipstitch in place, catching into the back of the machining to hide the stitches. If the heading is faced, slipstitch the lower edge of the facing in place.

FINISHING THE BINDING

Repeat this along the top and bottom edges of the curtain, but let the binding extend 1.5cm (⅝in) beyond either side of the curtain. After machining

the binding in place, fold these two extended pieces in so that they are enclosed when you fold the binding to the back. Then slipstitch these corners closed.

ADDING THE TIES

Fold the prepared ties in half and stitch them in place at 20cm (8in) intervals along the top, bound edge of the curtain. Tie on to the pole with a bow.

Right *The top edge of curtains with ties can be gathered for a fuller look or left ungathered. Here, lengths of narrow ribbon make a stylish alternative to fabric ties along the top edge of the curtain, and are tied directly on to the metal curtain pole.*

Above *Loops, or tabs, are an alternative to ties, and need to be placed on to the pole before it is fixed. Unlike ties, there is no room for adjustment, so if making your own tab-top curtains, make sure that the curtains and loops are the right length before hanging. Place the end loop beyond the wall bracket of the pole to anchor the curtain at the window edge when the curtain is drawn across.*

Lining curtains

LINING CURTAINS always improves their look. It helps them to hang better and to last longer since lining protects the main curtain fabric from dirt, fading and window condensation. The project below shows you the professional approach to lining curtains, where the two layers of fabric are locked together to improve the drape. You need a large work area. They are finished with the hand-pleated headings shown on pages 42–43.

Lining curtains

SUGGESTED FABRICS

Good-quality, luxurious fabrics; use cotton sateen in a neutral or dark colour for the linings

MATERIALS

Curtain fabric

Lining fabric

Lead curtain penny-weights (discs)

Vanishing marker or tailor's chalk

Scissors and sewing equipment

Matching sewing thread

MEASURING AND CUTTING OUT

Measure up, cut and join the fabric widths, allowing two times fullness; add 12.5cm (5in) to the width for turnings and 35.5cm (14in) to the length. Repeat for the lining fabric but don't add turning allowances.

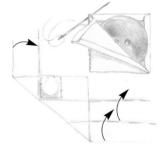

PRESSING THE SIDE AND LOWER HEM

Turn in the side seams of the curtain fabric by 6.5cm (2½in) and press. Turn up the bottom hem by 15cm (6in) and press. Open out the fold then press in half again to make a 7.5cm (3in) double hem. Unfold the side edge and the hem and fold the corner of the curtain towards the centre of the fabric at 45°. To fold at the correct point, insert a pin where the side fold and the innermost hem fold meet.

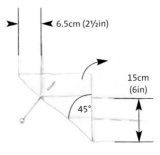

6.5cm (2½in)

15cm (6in)

45°

ATTACHING WEIGHTS

Cover each penny-weight with a small rectangle of lining fabric, turn in the raw edges and overstitch, then hand stitch the weights to the hem allowance.

STITCHING THE HEMS

Using sewing thread that matches the fabric, stitch the side seams in place using 5cm (2in) long herringbone stitches (see page 42). Slipstitch the curtain hem and the corner mitres.

ADDING THE LINING

Mark parallel lines down the length of the curtain 30–38cm (12–15in) apart. Lay the lining on top of the curtain, wrong sides together and with the raw edges level with the curtain's side and bottom edges. Pin the lining down the centre then fold back against the pins and lockstitch the lining to the curtain fabric (see page 69), beginning at the top and ending 10cm (4in) from the curtain hem's bottom. Repeat along the next marked line to one side of the centre

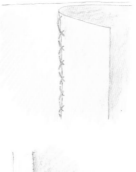

Above *Lining curtains and valances gives them a much better, finished look.*

and continue, working from the centre in both directions, until all is lockstitched.

FINISHING THE LINING

Make 2cm (¾in) turnings towards the wrong side along the lining's side seams, and turn under 5cm (2in) along the bottom edge. Press, pin and slipstitch in place.

Hand-pleated headings

HAND-PLEATED HEADINGS add a beautiful finishing touch to any curtain, especially those in rich fabrics that do not have over-fussy patterns. This phase of the project follows on from the professional method of making lined curtains described on pages 40–41.

Making hand-pleated headings

SUGGESTED FABRICS

Good-quality, luxurious fabrics

MATERIALS

Stitched curtains and linings from at the stage reached on pages 40–41

Vanishing marker or tailor's chalk

Heavyweight iron-on interfacing or 10cm (4in) wide buckram strips

Curtain or pin hooks

Scissors and sewing equipment

Matching sewing thread

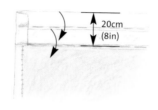

MAKING THE HEADING

Turn down 20cm (8in) from the top edge of the main fabric, press then open. Trim the lining level with this fold, then iron strips of interfacing (see page 68), 10cm (4in) deep, across the top flap of the curtain so that the bottom edge is level with the pressed fold. If using buckram, herringbone stitch it in place. Fold the top edge of the curtain fabric over the stiffening and fold again along the pressed fold to make a double hem. Baste across the curtain along the bottom edge of the stiffening; slipstitch the ends.

MARKING THE PLEATS

To calculate the goblet pleats, measure the curtain's width and halve it. Take away 5cm (2in) then divide the remainder into even widths of 10–15cm (4–6in). The number of even widths equals the number of pleats. The size of the width is the width of the pleat. To find the width of

the gap between pleats take half the width measurement of the curtain as before, take away 5cm (2in) and divide by the number of pleats minus one. Using tailor's chalk on the wrong side, mark a line at right-angles to the top edge, 5cm (2in) in from each side; it should run from the basting to the top of the fabric. Then mark a pleat width and a gap width, alternating the two across the top of the fabric.

STITCHING THE PLEATS AND ADDING HOOKS

Bring each pair of pleat lines together on the back of the

Left *Important windows deserve the hand-pleated treatment. Intricately sewn goblet headings ensure the full-length curtains at these tall windows hang well.*

Herringbone stitch

Herringbone stitch is both decorative and useful for a firm hem where you want a minimal bulk, for example, with very thick fabrics. Do not make an extra fold in the hem – simply neaten the fabric's raw edge with zigzag stitch before stitching the hem.

Working from left to right, bring the needle up through the hem, then insert it in the main fabric diagonally up to the right. Take a tiny stitch in the main fabric, then move the needle down diagonally to the right and take a stitch right through the hem. Then repeat this stitch all along the hem.

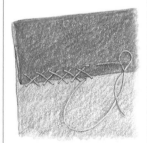

curtain to form a pleat. Stitch the pleat together on the right side, from top to bottom of the stiffening.

Pinch up the base of pleat along the basting line to form the goblet base. Stitch in place. Open out the top of the pleat and overstitch the back top edge to the top of the curtain, 12mm (½in) either side of the centre line.

To finish, stitch a curtain hook on the wrong side of each pleat or insert pin hooks, close to the top of the curtain.

Swags and tails

SWAGS AND TAILS give a much more formal look to curtains than a conventional pelmet. This treatment is best on larger windows since, not only is it meant to look grand, but it does reduce the light coming through the window, which is not so important if the windows are very large. Swags and tails are usually teamed with lined curtains with a pencil-pleat heading, although there are many style variations possible, some of which are less formal. The edges of swags and tails can be decorated with braid or fringing (see pages 60–61). Since the size of swags and tails depends on the size of the window, you will have to make your own pattern. For some styles, you will also need to fit a pelmet shelf with angle brackets (see page 71) so that the swags and tails can be fitted above it. If your window is very wide you may need more than one swag, in which case they should overlap by 10–15cm (4–6in).

Right *Swathes of fabric and clever combinations of colour and texture can create some dramatic looks. These swags and tails are trimmed with bullion fringing.*

Left *Swags and tails are most effective on long drapes in a formal, traditional setting. This swag-and-tail effect has been created using spiral hooks through which the ends of the fabric are pulled and secured to create 'puffs' of fabric each side.*

Below *Sophisticated window headings like this yellow and grey fabric draped around the curtain pole work best in larger rooms.*

Swag and tails on a pelmet shelf

SUGGESTED FABRICS

Good-quality curtain fabric that will drape well. Since the swag is cut on the diagonal, very bold designs or checks and stripes may not be suitable. The lining will show so choose it carefully to coordinate or contrast with your room scheme

MATERIALS

Curtain fabric for the swags and tails

Coordinating or contrasting lining fabric

Paper and pencil for making patterns

Spare fabric for testing out pattern

Drawing pins

Self-adhesive touch-and-close fastening or a staple gun

Scissors and sewing equipment

Matching sewing thread

Right *These tails have been hung so as to 'fall' down the front of the curtain. An alternative way of hanging tails is to fix them to the return of the pelmet shelf, which gives a slightly less formal effect.*

MAKING A PATTERN FOR THE SWAG

Measure the window and make a scale drawing, then sketch in the finished effect needed. The swag should drape no more than one-sixth of the way down the window. The inner length of the tails should be about the same as the finished centre depth of the swag, while the outer tail should come between about half to two-thirds of the way down the window.

Draw up your swag pattern. The top edge should be about 40cm (16in) narrower than the shelf width (the swag ends need to be hidden under the tails) and the lower edge about 20cm (8in) longer than the shelf, although this will depend on the window proportions and the drape wanted.

For your lower edge measurement, hold a tape measure down in a loop from one corner of the shelf to the other until you like the effect. The pattern length for the swag should be two and a half times the finished length to allow for pleats, and the widest point (the lower edge measurement) three-quarters of the way down the pattern.

Round off the bottom quarter of the swag to form an even curve. For the pleats, mark an even number of points down the sloping sides of the pattern, spaced roughly every 10–15cm (4–6in).

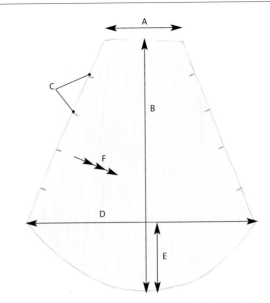

A 40cm (16in) narrower than pelmet shelf
B 2½ x finished length
C Pleat points
D 20cm (8in) longer than pelmet shelf
E ¼ x pattern length
F Straight grain of fabric

TESTING THE SWAG PATTERN

Cut out a trial swag from your spare fabric, turning the pattern through 45° to cut the shape on the bias. Pleat the side edges by bringing the lowest point to the next, then that point to the one above and so on. Pin the pleats in place then fix the trial swag to the pelmet shelf temporarily with drawing pins. Adjust the pleats if necessary.

CUTTING OUT

When you have the effect you want, add a 1.5cm (⅝in) seam allowance all round and cut one swag from the curtain fabric and one from the lining fabric – cutting both of them on the bias.

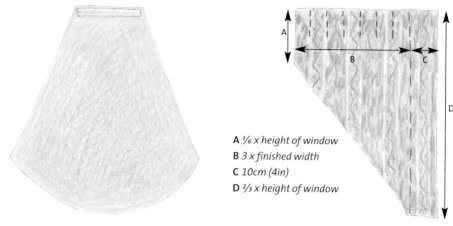

A 1/6 x height of window
B 3 x finished width
C 10cm (4in)
D 2/3 x height of window

MAKING THE SWAG

Pin the swag pieces together, right sides facing, and stitch around all the edges, leaving a top gap for turning the fabric the right side out. Trim the seams, clip the curves and corners and turn the right side out and press. Slipstitch the opening closed. Machine stitch the 'sew' half of the touch-and-close tape along the back top edge of the swag.

Right *Two-tone swags can be made by stitching a strip of the curtain fabric along the bottom edge of a coordinating plain fabric swag, as shown here. Swags are usually cut on the bias, but if you are using striped or other obviously directional fabric you will need to cut them on the straight grain.*

Pleat the swag as before, using pins. Stick the adhesive side of the touch-and-close fastening to the top of the pelmet shelf and press the swag in place. (If using a staple gun, hold the swag in place with drawing pins temporarily.) When satisfied, baste then machine stitch down each sloping edge to hold the pleats in place. Press or staple the swag in position.

MAKING A PATTERN FOR THE TAILS

Make this pattern, following the proportions in 'Making a pattern for the swag' (see page 47). Decide on the desired finished width and triple it, then add a return of 10cm (4in) – the depth of the pelmet from front to back.

TESTING THE TAILS PATTERN

Cut left- and right-hand tails on the straight grain from your trial fabric. Pleat the sloping sections and pin each in place. Fix to the shelf with drawing pins, with the return sections along its ends. The tails should hide the ends of the swag.

CUTTING OUT

When satisfied with the shape of the tails and the pleating, add a 1.5cm (5/8in) seam allowance all round plus 10cm (4in) at the top for fixing it to the pelmet shelf. Cut out a left and a right tail from the curtain fabric, on the straight grain, reversing the

pattern to cut the second piece. Then cut left and right linings in the same way.

MAKING THE TAILS

Pin each piece of curtain fabric to its lining, right sides facing; stitch and turn the right side out as for the swag. Pleat up the tails, pinning the pleats in place, and position the tails on the pelmet shelf as before to check. If satisfactory, machine stitch along the top edge to hold the pleats in place. Stitch touch-and-close fastening

to the top back edges of the tails and stick the other strip to the top of the pelmet shelf as before. Press the tails in place on the pelmet shelf over the swag.

Above *A swag-and-tail effect is a good decorative option in a recessed window with no room for curtains. Here, panels of contrasting fabrics have been sewn back to back, draped over painted wooden curtain hold-backs at the top of the window and tied with narrow ribbon.*

Bed curtains

YOU CAN DECORATE a bedhead with many devices – from simple wall hangings (rugs or quilts hung on the wall above the bed) to half-testers and elaborate coronets strung from the ceiling or the wall. The fixture you choose will dictate the bed curtain heading and lining.

Historical influences

Bed curtains were used for privacy and to keep out draughts long before curtains were hung at windows. In medieval and Tudor times wool drapes kept out prying eyes in a time when there were no room partitions.

By the 18th century four-poster beds were going out of fashion and, instead, beds were given decorative drapes that hung from the ceiling or wall. The Victorians briefly reintroduced the four-poster but decided that it was not healthy to enclose the bed with curtains, so they chose the half-tester instead. This was a canopy over the head end of the bed only, designed to keep out draughts. The four-poster is now under-going another revival and decorative bed drapes are currently very fashionable.

Contemporary styles

The easiest way to add style and interest to a bed is to display a rug, patchwork quilt or unusual panel of fabric on the wall behind the bedhead. Another simple approach is to drape muslin, mosquito-net style, from a ceiling hook above the bed. Alternatively, you can fit a coronet on the wall above the bedhead. This is a semicircular pelmet from which drapes are hung. These drapes usually need to be lined, preferably with a contrasting fabric, and are held either side of the bedhead with hold-backs. Half-testers are similar to coronets, but the pelmet, often decorative, is rectangular. Again, the drapes are usually lined.

Dressing four-poster beds is dictated to some extent by the bed's style. With a modern design, muslin can be draped over the canopy (a piece of fabric that ties to the top of the frame).

Or go for dress curtains at each corner, a canopy, tie-backs and a matching bed valance and comforter. Bound-edge curtains (see pages 36–37) look good on contemporary four-poster beds.

Traditional-style four-posters can have the complete look: generous, full-length, lined curtains with braid and fringed edges, sumptuous tie-backs, a canopy and pelmet, matching bed valance, contrasting lightweight curtains, plus coordinated bedding.

Above *Four-poster beds demand generous quantities of fabric and trimmings.*

Left *Sheer, translucent fabrics are ideal for bed hangings, supported by a simple hoop.*

Right *Although elaborate bed coronets are usually lined, less formal examples, like this one over a child's bed, can be made from unlined fabric, provided it looks the same on both sides.*

Sheer curtains

SHEER FABRICS – net, voile, lace and muslin – have become a very important part of window treatments. They are no longer just for privacy; laces and voiles can look romantic or stylish as they billow in the breeze on a summer's day, and most furnishing fabric manufacturers now offer coordinating sheers as part of their ranges.

Modern sheers come in many different textures, designs and fabric types and in a variety of colours and effects. They can play a stunning part in a multi-layered look and, for traditional, period-style rooms, off-white cotton lace can be bought in wonderful authentic Victorian designs.

Right *Sheer fabrics allow a beautiful diffused light into a room and make a stunning window covering, provided privacy and draughts are not a problem. In winter you can always add a blind or change them for warmer curtains.*

Decorative ideas

- You can make tie-backs from patterned fabric and add a border strip of the same fabric along the bottom edges of the curtains to coordinate.

- If you use plain sheers, you could add a trimming of lace or fringing along the hem and along the long side edges that meet in the centre of the window, which will show best when the curtains are held back to the sides of the window with hold-backs or tie-backs.

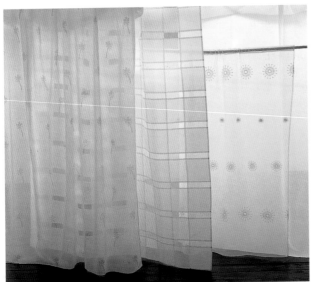

Left and below left *There is a huge choice of coloured and printed voiles and semi-translucent fabrics available, some of which come with matching curtain fabric.*

Sheer tips

- At night, when the lights are on in a room, sheer fabrics offer no privacy. If you are overlooked, combine them with blinds or conventional curtains.

- You can buy transparent curtain tape for sheer fabrics, and also special lightweight track or expanding poles, which give a more professional look than old-fashioned stretch wires.

- Avoid making joins in sheer fabrics. You can hang widths next to each other without sewing as the fullness of the curtains will usually disguise the overlap. If you have to join sheers use flat fell seams (see page 65).

- Use sharp scissors when cutting sheer fabric and a fine, sharp needle in your sewing machine to avoid snagging.

Double sheer curtains

SUGGESTED FABRICS

The fabric must be reversible and the design must be the same in both directions. Also, look for fabric with a neat selvage that will not need hemming

MATERIALS

Voile, lace or other sheer fabric

Expanding net pole for fitting curtains inside window recess, or a fitted curtain pole (see pages 20–21) without the curtain rings

Scissors and sewing equipment

Matching sewing thread

These overlapping voile curtains are easy to make and can be either used on their own or teamed with a blind or conventional curtains for privacy. All turnings must be neat and straight as they will be seen through the fabric.

MEASURING UP AND CALCULATING FABRIC

Measure up to determine the quantity of fabric required for the curtains (see pages 16–19), allowing twice the width of the pole for fullness. For recess fitting, double the length of the window and add 7.5cm (3in) for hems. If the curtains are to be hung outside the recess, decide how long you want them to be then measure from the top of the pole to the bottom of the intended drop, double this then add a further 7.5cm (3in) for hems.

Right *These simple double sheer curtains use swathes of inexpensive fabric in a lightly woven check to create a luxurious and romantic effect.*

FITTING THE DRAPES

Fold the fabric in half, drape it over the pole and pin it underneath. The casing must be deep enough to allow you to slide the pole in easily, but not so deep that it will look baggy.

MAKING THE CASING

Measure the depth of the casing, remove the fabric from the pole, measure up again to check that the casing is straight, baste and then stitch in position.

MAKING THE HEMS

Thread the curtain pole, if using, through the casing and check the length of the curtain. Then fold up a double hem on each fabric length, making sure that the two parts of the hem are the same depth.

Make sure the hem is straight, as this is also seen from the right side. Both hems must be folded towards the window side. Machine or hand stitch the hems.

HANGING THE CURTAIN

Hang the curtain (or fit on a net pole, if using), then fit hold-backs or tie-backs two-thirds of the way down the sides of the window (see pages 28–31) and drape the front piece of fabric over one and the back piece of fabric over the other.

Above *There are hundreds of ways of dressing windows with sheer fabrics. Here five lengths of voile have been hung over a curtain pole, one swept to each side, two knotted loosely and one left to hang straight.*

Blinds

BLINDS LOOK NEAT and stylish and are very useful in small rooms where curtains may be overpowering, and for windows where there is little space to the side for curtains. Blinds are economical on fabric; they work well as part of a layered look and are great for showing off bold patterns because when the blinds are lowered the fabric lies flat. Blinds made of sheer fabrics are useful for providing privacy yet allowing light to filter into the room.

Wide windows are best treated with two or more blinds side by side, since one very wide one could prove awkward to operate.

Blinds may sound a little complicated to make but they really are quite easy. The roller blind, which relies on a sprung roller to raise the blind, can be made with a kit. Roman blinds are the most elegant of the flat-faced blinds, and complement almost any decorative scheme. The Roman blind in the project opposite has dowels to ensure that the blind folds up neatly when raised and needs to be fixed to a batten, which is then fixed above the window.

Above *Making your own roller blinds is easy when using a kit with all the components. Apply stiffener to untreated fabric, following the manufacturer's instructions.*

Right *The position of this window directly behind the kitchen sink means that a simple roller blind is more suitable than curtains, which would get in the way of washing up and become dirty very quickly.*

Making a Roman blind

SUGGESTED FABRICS

Good-quality fabrics, with firm, straight weave. Any pattern must be printed squarely on the fabric grain

MATERIALS

Main fabric for blind

Suitable lining fabric

Pencil or dressmaking marker

Scissors and sewing equipment

Matching sewing thread

Several strips of fine dowelling 3cm (1¼in) less than the blind's width

A wooden lath, 2cm (¾in) shorter than the finished blind width

Small brass or nylon blind rings – two or more for each dowel

A staple gun and staples or small flat-topped nails and a hammer

Small screw-eyes

Fine nylon blind cord

Wooden or nylon blind acorn

Basic DIY tool kit

Small angle irons and screws or masonry screws and wallplugs

Cleat to take blind cord

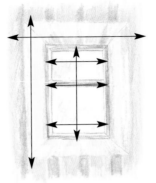

MEASURING AND CUTTING OUT

For a blind hung inside the window recess, measure the width of the recess in several places and deduct 1cm (⅜in) from the smallest measurement for clearance. This is the blind's finished width. If the blind is to hang outside the recess or on a flush-fitting window (i.e. surface-mounted), measure window's width, adding 5cm (2in) for the finished blind width, then add 9cm (3½in) to the blind's width (for turnings) for your fabric width. Measure from the top of the window to the sill for the blind's finished length. Add 12.5cm (5in) for turnings and hems. Add an extra 5cm (2in) if surface-mounting your blind. Cut the fabric to size. Cut the lining to the same length as the top fabric and the same width, less 12cm (4¾in). You will need extra lining for the dowel casings.

MAKING UP THE BLIND

Lay the top fabric on the lining, right sides facing and raw edges level top and bottom. Pin the side seams with the raw edges level. Machine stitch together with a 1.5cm (⅝in) seam. Press the seam open and turn the tube of fabric right side out. Working with the lining uppermost, press the outside edges so that an equal margin of top fabric shows on either side. Baste down and across the centres to hold the two layers together.

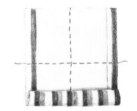

FINISHING THE LOWER EDGE

Turn the fabric and lining under by 12mm (½in) along the bottom edge, towards the lining, and press. Turn under another 7cm (2¾in) for a casing. Machine stitch close to the fold.

MAKING DOWEL CASINGS

Cut pieces of lining fabric the same width as the finished blind width and 5cm (2in) deep for the dowel casings. The number depends on the blind's length: you will need one pocket every 20–25cm (8–10in). Mark lengthways along the centre line of each lining strip with a pencil or dressmaking marker. Press in 1cm (³⁄₈in) along the long edges and short ends. Temporarily mark a line across the back of the blind for each dowel. Space the lines evenly down the blind with an even gap top and bottom. Pin a lining strip to every line on your blind, matching up the marked lines and 1cm (³⁄₈in) in from the blind's edges.

FITTING THE DOWELS

Machine stitch each strip in place along the lines. Fold each strip in half along the centre line and hand or machine stitch close to the folded long edges. Slide a

dowel into each of the pockets and slipstitch both ends. Slide the lath into the bottom casing and slipstitch the ends. Remove the basting. Stitch two rings to each dowel pocket, 2cm (³⁄₄in) in from the sides of the blind. Unless the blind is quite narrow, add one or more vertical rows of rings in between. Space them out evenly, about 25–30cm (10–12in) apart.

FINISHING THE TOP EDGE

Fold 4.5cm (1³⁄₄in) of the top of the blind over the edge of the batten to be fitted on the wall. Fix with a staple gun or small,

Above *A Roman blind in a modern fabric makes an eye-catching feature in a bathroom that combines old and new styles.*

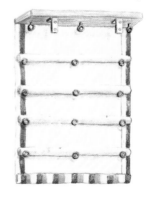

flat-topped nails. Ensure that the blind is square on the batten so that it will hang straight.

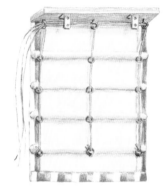

CORDING THE BLIND

Fix a screw-eye into the under-side of the batten above each vertical row of rings. To calculate the blind cord needed, double the blind's length, add the distance between left- and right-hand rows of rings and multiply by the number of vertical rows of rings. Cut the cord into equal lengths, one for each vertical row of rings. Decide which side of the window to hang the pull-cord. Thread each cord vertically through each row of rings and then through the screw eye at the top of the row. Tie the cord to the bottom ring of each row; thread each cord through previous screw-eyes to the eye at the side where the pull cord is to be. Gather the cords hanging at the side, trim to the same length and thread on to the acorn. Knot the cords just above the sill and slide the acorn over the knot.

FIXING THE BLIND IN PLACE

Fix the batten over the window frame using angle irons, or screw through the batten upward into the window reveal. Fix the cleat for the cord to the wall beside the window or in the reveal. When the blind is raised, wind the cord around the cleat.

Below *This elaborate 'pull-up' blind is a variation on the Roman blind, and based on the type often used in Georgian times.*

JOINING FABRIC WIDTHS

If your main or lining fabrics are too narrow for the window, join the lengths together. Add 3cm (1¼in) to your fabric width for every join. Make any joins either in the centre or equally spaced to either side of the centre point, taking a 1.5cm (⅝in) seam. Match any repeats – you may need some extra fabric for this (see page 63). Press the seams open.

Braids and trimmings

BRAIDS AND TRIMMINGS can add something special to curtains and blinds. They should coordinate and enhance a window feature, not dominate. Avoid heavy or skimpy fabric edgings, and if you are going to use them around curves make sure they are flexible. Many soft furnishing manufacturers offer ranges of cord, ready-covered piping, bullion fringing and bobble trim to coordinate with their fabrics. These beautiful modern designs and colourways are very different from the traditional, heavy-looking Victorian braids and trimmings. Trimmings can be expensive so work out exactly what you need before buying. They need to be applied carefully to achieve the best effect.

Above *Braids and trimmings are back in fashion and manufacturers are producing stunning ranges of designs to coordinate with their furnishing fabric ranges.*

Left *Bobble trim is very effective along the edges of curtains or the bottom of blinds, showing up in silhouette against the light from the window.*

Right *Ready-made tassels give a distinctive, sometimes theatrical, touch to curtain tie-backs. Use elaborately woven cords with luxurious fabrics, or simpler styles with plain cottons and linens.*

Applying braids and trimmings

topstitching. If hand stitching, use tiny invisible slipstitches. Turn under the cut ends of braid by 6mm (¼in) before sewing to stop them unravelling.

ATTACHING CORD
Stitch cord on to the edge of curtains, fabric pelmets, tie-backs and drapes by taking an invisible stitch along the folded edge of the curtain, then along the inside of the cord and back along the curtain edge.

FIXING BRAID
Braid is usually sewn close to the finished edges of curtains, swags, tails, fabric pelmets and blinds. Alternatively, it can be

inset from the edge slightly to create a strong border. Machine or hand stitch braid along both sides. Some braids will be flattened by machining, while others are too bulky to go beneath the presser foot at all, so experiment with an off-cut of braid and material first.

If machine sewing is acceptable, sew both sides in the same direction to avoid puckering. Mitre the corners of braid and baste it in place before

ADDING FRINGING
Covered piping and some fringing can be sandwiched on the inside edge of seams where the lining is the same size as the main fabric – such as with swags and tails – while sewing. Baste the braid in place to the right side of the fabric along the seam line, but take care not to catch the fringing in the stitching. As with piping (see page 67), when the fabric is turned the right side out the piping or fringing is on the outside edge.

Practicalities

FOR SUCCESSFUL blind- and curtain-making, it is worth learning some of the sewing tips and techniques that will give your window treatments that coveted professional finish. The following pages cover seams and hems, as well as other practical matters, such as pattern matching and careful pressing. Knowing how to use interfacing and interlinings, which stiffen fabrics and provide extra body, respectively, is useful. Piping is another little extra – it looks fancy but is incredibly easy to make and is effective on tailored tie-backs, for example. Lastly, it is worth being aware of the many fixtures and fittings available for displaying the curtains and blinds in your home.

Cutting fabric

WHATEVER TYPE of curtains or blind you embark upon making, you will need to cut out panels of fabric. You might need to match patterns if you are using a patterned fabric and you will certainly need to press seams and panels of fabric for a professional finish.

Cutting out curtains

You will need a large, clean and clear surface on which you can lay your fabric flat for cutting. This can be a sturdy table or even the floor if you do not have a large table. If you are using a table, it should be at least as wide as the fabric you are using.

- For details of how to calculate the size of the fabric panels required, see pages 16–19. Work out your calculations on paper and draw a diagram to show how the fabric widths fit together.

- Measure out the first drop and draw a cutting line with tailor's chalk exactly at right angles to the selvage.

- Cut the length and write 'top' on the back of the top edge with tailor's chalk. Repeat the process for the number of drops required.

- If you are working with a patterned fabric, check that you always position the same part of the pattern at the top of the panel of fabric. If the patterned fabric has a half drop, check that the pattern matches down the side edges that are to be joined.

- Trim away the selvages, or at least clip them every 10cm (4in). The selvages are woven more tightly than the rest of the fabric, so if you do not do this the fabric may pucker and the curtains may not hang properly.

- Lay out the drops so that you have two curtains of equal width. If you have an odd number of drops, cut one in half lengthways. Position these halves on the outer edges of the whole drops.

Pressing and ironing

Do not regard the iron as something you use only after making curtains. Pressing is an integral part of good curtain-making.

Ironing helps to remove wrinkles and creases from fabric. Pressing, however, is a more precise technique: working on a small area at a time, you use the heat and steam from an iron to flatten details, lifting the iron up and down. Use the point of the iron to get into corners.

After stitching a straight seam, press along the line of stitching, to set the stitches into the fabric, then open out the seam and press the seam allowance open from the wrong side.

Pattern matching

When joining panels of fabric to make curtains, ensure that you match the pattern along seam lines, particularly with bold patterns on large curtains. Allow a slight margin of error when cutting out the fabric, then join the widths of fabric, as follows.

Press under the seam allowance of one fabric piece, then position it on the second piece so that you can see the right side of both pieces to be joined. Move the folded edge over the other piece until the pattern matches. Pin the seam allowances together from beneath the fabric, then stitch and trim any excess fabric.

Seams

MOST SEWING involves seams. For curtains and blinds, these are mostly long straight seams. Some seams are decorative, while others need to be invisible. For strength, most seams are stitched by machine, but in some cases you may prefer to sew by hand, using a fine running stitch or backstitch.

Before machine stitching a seam, match the edges to be joined carefully, with right sides facing, and pin the layers together close to the stitching line. Position your pins at right angles to the stitching lines, so that the points just reach the seam line. If you prefer, baste the layers together before stitching the seam.

Flat seams

A flat seam is commonly used for joining fabric widths such as those needed for curtains.

To make a seam lie flat and prevent unsightly lumps on the right side of the fabric, you may need to trim and layer the seam allowance, particularly if there are several layers of fabric. If this is the case, trim each layer a different amount, so that the edges do not all fall together when the seam is pressed. Also trim, notch and clip the seam allowances of curved seams and at corners, so that when the piece is turned the right side out, you will have a smooth unpuckered curve or a crisp corner. You can also neaten the edges of a seam allowance by trimming it with pinking shears, with a zigzag or overlock stitch, by turning under and stitching the raw edges or, with a heavy fabric, you may prefer to bind the raw edges with bias binding.

STITCHING A FLAT SEAM

Stitch the seam with the fabric's right sides together and raw edges matching. Normally, a 1.5cm (⅝in) seam allowance is used. Reinforce the ends of the seam line by reverse stitching.

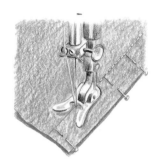

CLIPPING CORNERS

On a stitched corner, clip away the seam allowance diagonally across the corner. For particularly bulky and sharply angled corners, you can taper the seam allowances further, to reduce the thickness of the fabric in the corner when the item is turned the right side out.

CLIPPING AND NOTCHING CURVED SEAMS

On an outer curve, on a swag for example, cut little notches out of the seam allowances every 2.5–5cm (1–2in) so that when the piece is turned the right side out the fabric lies flat. On inner curves, clip into the seam allowance, so that when the item is the right side out the outer edges of the seam allowance lie flat.

Flat fell seam

A flat fell, or run-and-fell, seam is a flat seam that encloses the fabric's raw edges without creating too much of a ridge in the fabric along the seam line. The seam is highlighted with a line of stitching running down beside it. On the back of the seam, you can see two parallel lines of stitching. It is useful for joining seams that will be under strain, and for seams that may be seen from either side – on unlined curtains, for example.

STITCHING A FLAT FELL SEAM

Stitch a normal seam, with the right sides of the fabric together and raw edges matching. Press the seam, press it open, then press both seam allowances to one side. Trim the seam allowance pressed closest to the fabric to 1cm (⅜in) then turn under 6mm (¼in) along the uppermost seam allowance. Pin and baste the upper seam allowance to the fabric, enclosing the raw edges of the lower

seam allowance. Topstitch the length of the seam close to the folded edge.

Lapped and butt seams

Lapped seams are simple seams, used to join fabric widths that will not fray or that will be enclosed in the item. The seams create minimal bulk, and are useful for joining widths of interlining that will be enclosed in a curtain. The seam allowances can be trimmed after stitching. If the layers of fabric are particularly bulky, for example when joining widths of wadding in large, quilted panels, they can be joined with a butt seam: the edges of the fabric are joined by hand without overlapping them at all.

JOINING INTERLINING OR WADDING

To join layers of wadding or interlining with minimal bulk,

use a wide or multi-zigzag stitch. Overlap the seam allowances, machine stitch with zigzag stitch and then trim away the excess fabric.

For bulky layers of wadding or very thick interlining, butt together the edges that are to be joined, and stitch by hand with herringbone stitch (see page 42), taking stitches across the join on alternate sides.

Lapped seam for non-fray fabrics

When joining PVC or felt, for minimal bulk, overlap the two edges to be joined by a total of 3cm (1¼in) and, with right sides uppermost, stitch along the seam line. If the seam will be subject to wear and tear, make a second row of stitching 12mm (½in) from the first. Trim the seam allowances close to the rows of stitching.

Hems

THE EDGES of most soft furnishings have to be carefully finished to ensure that they look good and do not fray when laundered. The options are to hem the edge or to bind it with a matching or contrasting fabric.

Hems are generally intended to provide an almost invisible finish to the edge of an item. The traditional dressmaker's hem involves a narrow turning, and then a deeper turning which can be adjusted at the final fitting stage. Most hems or edges in home sewing, however, are double hems, with two equal turnings, to give a crisper finish. Hems can be stitched in place by hand for an invisible finish (see page 33), by machine using a special hemming stitch or they can be topstitched by machine.

Mitring hems

One problem area with hems lies in getting a neat finish at corners on square items. To finish corners neatly, the hems have to be folded to create a diagonal pleat – a procedure known as mitring. At the same time, excess fabric is trimmed away so that the corners lie flat and are not lumpy.

TRIMMING THE FABRIC
Unfold the pressed fabric. Trim away the fabric across the corner, cutting 3mm (⅛in) diagonally outward from the point where the fold lines cross. Press under a 3mm (⅛in) turning across the corner.

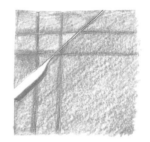

FOLDING THE MITRE
Refold the first turning of the hem, keeping the diagonal turning in place. Turn under the second fold of the hem and the edges of the diagonal turning should meet neatly at the corner. Baste in place then machine or hand stitch.

PRESSING A HEM TO BE MITRED
Where the hem goes around a corner, whether stitching the hem by hand or machine, you must reduce the fabric's bulk by mitring for a neat finish. First press the turning allowance and the hem all round the edge of the item. This will ensure that the material is flat and the cut accurate.

Hemstitch
Hemstitch alternates three straight stitches with a zigzag stitch, which just catches a couple of threads of the main fabric. Press the hem in place, then fold back the fabric where the hem's fold is to be stitched to the main part of the work. Stitch along the folded hemline, catching a couple of threads of fabric as the machine needle swings to the side.

Piping

STRAIGHT SEAMS and hems should usually be as invisible as possible in many soft furnishings. However, you can make a feature of seams with piping, which outlines items such as cushions and fitted sofa covers in order to emphasize their shape.

In curtain-making, piping is particularly useful when making tailored tie-backs (see page 31). Even if a pattern does not give specific instructions for including piping, this simple decoration can be fitted relatively easily into almost any flat seam.

Making piping

Piping requires strips of fabric cut on the bias, known as bias strips or bias binding. To cover piping cord, you will need 4–5cm (1½–2in) wide strips, depending on the fabric weight and the size of the piping cord to be covered. This provides for a 1.5cm (⅝in) seam allowance, plus fabric to wrap around the cord.

Piping cord is usually made of cotton and should be preshrunk (or wash it before use) if you are inserting it in an item that is washable.

Measure the width of the binding at right angles to this first line, then mark in the bias strips parallel to the first line. Cut out along the marked lines to give the number of strips that you require.

MARKING AND CUTTING BIAS STRIPS

Take a rectangle of fabric and mark a diagonal, at a 45° angle to the selvage, from one corner across to the opposite edge.

JOINING BIAS STRIPS

Position two strips, right sides together, at right angles, their raw edges meeting. Overlap the pieces so that the corners extend on either side and you can make a seam line running from edge to edge and 1cm (⅜in) from the raw edges. Press the stitching, then press the seam open and trim away the corners. Wrap the bias strips around the piping cord, then stitch as close as possible to the cord, through both fabric layers.

STITCHING PIPING IN PLACE

Position the covered piping on the right side of one piece of fabric, so that the piping stitching line matches the fabric's seam line and the raw edge of the piping covering is towards the raw edge of the fabric. Stitch in place, then position the second panel of fabric on top of the piping, right side inward, and stitch again. If the piping goes around a gently curved corner, make several cuts into the seam allowance so that you can ease it into position.

Interfacings and interlinings

INTERFACINGS AND INTERLININGS give home sewing a professional finish. There are many ways in which you can improve a finished soft furnishing project by adding extra hidden layers as you make up the item. Interfacings can stiffen fabrics and give a crisp finish, while interlinings are soft fabrics that give extra body to soft furnishings.

Choosing and using interfacings

Interfacings are ideal stiffening for fabrics in curtain headings and pelmets and for items such as tailored tie-backs. Traditional interfacings are woven, but modern non-woven interfacings are easier to work with and often come with a special backing so that they can be ironed on to the main fabric.

Most interfacings are sold in black, white or neutral colours.

- Buckram is a traditional, very stiff interfacing. It is available in narrow strips – convenient for a crisp finish along the top of a curtain. It can also back pelmets to give a tailored look to window top.

- Purpose-made stiffening for curtain headings is available in convenient widths.

- Purpose-made, non-woven interfacings in different weights, with or without an iron-on backing, can also be used instead of traditional interfacings. Because they have no grain, they do not have to be aligned with the fabric to match the weave when cutting out. The

interfacing is usually trimmed away close to the stitching before finishing the project, to reduce the seam bulk.

USING IRON-ON INTERFACING
Always press the fabric to be interfaced carefully before fusing interfacing, and apply the interfacing to the fabric's wrong side. To protect the sole plate of the iron and to ensure the iron does not over-heat the fusible (iron-on) interfacing, use a pressing cloth between the iron and the interfacing.

APPLYING LIGHTWEIGHT SEW-IN INTERFACING
Cut the interfacing to the same size as the main fabric piece to be faced, and baste the inter-facing to the wrong side. Use the two fabric layers as though they

were a single layer. Trim away all the interfacing from the seam allowances, close to the seam line, after finishing the seam.

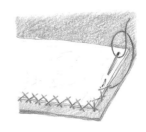

USING SEW-IN INTERFACING
When using very heavy, stiff interfacing, trim all seam allowances, plus an extra 3–6mm ($\frac{1}{8}$–$\frac{1}{4}$in) from the outer edge of interfacing. Position the interfacing on the wrong side of the fabric and secure it with herringbone stitch (see page 42), picking up only a single thread from the main fabric as you stitch over the edge of the facing.

Interlinings

Interlining is a layer of soft fabric, caught between the main fabric and lining, which gives a luxurious finish and helps to improve a curtain's drape. Traditional interlinings include bump and domette, which are used in curtains. Flannelette and synthetic wadding (available with iron-on backing for quilted projects) can also be used. When choosing an interlining, check whether it will wash (or dry clean) with the fabric used. The colour choice is often even more restricted than with interfacing.

Interlining is a bulky fabric, so join widths by machine with lapped seams (see page 65), or by hand with herringbone stitch (see page 42) to prevent any stiffness at the join. Once the item is made up, the interlining is enclosed by the main fabric and lining, so its raw edges are protected from fraying.

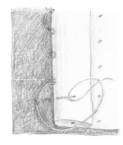

LOCKING IN INTERLINING
To prevent interlining slipping around inside curtains, lock it to the wrong side of the main fabric before making up the curtains. Lockstitch is a long, looped stitch, worked down the length of the curtain on a fold in the interlining. Pick up only a single thread of the curtain fabric and do not pull the thread taut.

Heavy self-adhesive stiffening
Projects such as shaped fabric pelmets and tie-backs are easier if you use self-adhesive stiffening. The card can be cut to the shape required, then the backing is removed and the adhesive side covered with fabric. When sticking fabric to self-adhesive card, work from one end to the other, smoothing the fabric to remove wrinkles.

Below *A selection of interfacings and stiffenings, used to give a crisp finish to soft furnishing projects, ranging from very stiff buckram, through assorted weights of non-woven iron-on and sew-in interfacing to the very fine organdie and marquisette, used for appliqué or embroidery work.*

Fixings and fittings

YOU CANNOT HANG CURTAINS, blinds and drapes without some sort of track or pole running across the window. The actual fixing method depends on the surface you are fixing into and the brackets supplied with the track, rod or pole. If you are fitting ready-made blinds, these are usually supplied complete with a heading box, which is held in place at each end.

How will the track or pole be fixed?

Start by taking a good look at the wall or ceiling above the window you are dressing. The window may be in an alcove, you may want to fit a track or pole to the wall above the window, or it may be easier to fit it to the ceiling.

Houses built from a timber frame construction have hollow (stud) walls, with a plasterboard surface supported on upright studs every 30–38cm (12–15in) across the wall. You can make a safer fixing if you drill into one of these studs, or into the wooden framework surrounding the window. You can then use wood screws to screw the brackets in place. You could use plasterboard fixings, but only if the pole and fabric are light.

It may be easier to fit a wooden batten above the window, painted or papered to match the wall, so that you can fit the brackets supporting the rods at any point across the top of the window. This also applies if the walls are uneven, or the plaster is old.

Solid walls need drilling and fitting with wallplugs that will hold fast the screws for brackets and tracks.

BLOCKS FOR PLASTIC TRACKS
Plastic blocks for some tracks can be screwed either into the wall, directly into the ceiling or into a wall-mounted batten.

METAL POLES
For most systems, there are only a few types of brackets available to support the poles, so choose finials to make a style statement.

Check whether you need a central bracket to provide support for a long pole, and that there is a suitable point on the wall or window frame where you are able to fix it.

LIGHTWEIGHT CEILING TRACKS
This simple plastic track can be screwed into the ceiling. Runners slot into the track, but they are only ever suitable for use with lightweight drapes.

WOODEN POLES AND BRACKETS
Brackets for wooden poles are available in different lengths to adjust the curtain depth from the window. The brackets should be fitted about 5cm (2in) from the end of the pole (excluding the finial) so that there is room for a single ring between the bracket and the finial. This anchors the curtain when you

draw it across. Very long poles will require central brackets, too, for strength. The brackets can also be hung from the ceiling. Wooden sockets are available if the curtain pole is to be fitted in a recess.

can buy surface-mounted end sockets if the rod is to be fitted on the wall surface or attached to the window surround.

finishes for telescopic rods include plain white plastic, aluminium and brass.

RODS AND SOCKETS
Brass and other lightweight rods are suitable for placing inside a recess. Sockets can be fitted on each end, which are then screwed into the sides of the recess. Or, if you prefer, you

TELESCOPIC RODS
Some shower curtain fittings and lightweight curtain rods are telescopic. Buy them slightly longer than the recess they are to fit into, and put them in position: a spring inside pushes the ends out against the sides of the recess and there is no drilling or screwing required. Common

CURTAIN WIRES
Plastic-covered sprung curtain wires, again suitable only for holding lightweight curtains, are looped on to screw-eyes fitted at either end of a surface or recess. Screw-eyes are suitable only for fixing into wooden surrounds.

Wooden pelmet shelves
Pelmet shelves have several advantages. They provide a secure fixing point for curtain tracks or poles, as well as for decorative fabric pelmets, valances or elaborate swags and tails (see pages 46–49), while hiding the curtain track or pole, protecting it and the heading from dust.

Use planed timber (PAR, planed all round), about 12mm (½in) thick and 10cm (4in) wide, depending on the window's size and the weight of the curtains. The shelf should extend about 6.5cm (2½in) beyond the window at either end.

Angle irons, L-shaped metal plates with two holes in each leg, are a convenient way of fixing the shelf. Screw one side into the underside of the shelf, then hold the shelf in position above

the window and mark drilling points on the wall through the angle iron's remaining holes. Position the angle irons every 20cm (8in) along the shelf's length. If the shelf is flush with the top of the window recess, angle irons may be fitted above the shelf.

Alternatively screw a wooden batten, the same length as the shelf, to the wall above the window and screw the shelf into the top of the batten, close to the wall. For a sturdier construction, fix front and end panels to the edges of the shelf. The bottom edges of these can be shaped decoratively before assembly.

Once the pelmet shelf is up, attach a fabric pelmet, valance or swag to the front, and fit a track or pole for curtains to the underside.

Fitting the track or pole and hanging the curtains

Careful marking and secure fixing are vital for long-lasting, good-looking curtain tracks and poles. Get the right tools for the job, and measure and mark before screwing the brackets for a curtain pole or the block supports for track in place.

Once these are in place, fit the curtain track and runners or pole and rings. You need enough curtain hooks and runners or rings to position them 5–7.5cm (2–3in) apart across the width of the curtain, with one at each end. The heavier the curtains, the more hooks you will need. Pinch-pleated curtains should be hung from a hook at each pleat.

- Plastic tracks usually clip on to block supports, but with some track systems you have to slide the track on to the supports before you screw them in place, so do check this first.

- Curtain rods and poles usually slot through the brackets, but some rest in cup-shaped brackets.

- Ensure you have enough runners or rings slotted in place before fixing (to save stretching into awkward corners). With rods and poles, leave two rings off, fit the pole so that most of the rings are between the brackets, then add a reserved ring between each end bracket and finial. Placing these rings here anchors the curtain for when you draw it across.

- With the curtains laid out flat, insert hooks into the curtain tape, positioning a hook at the end of each curtain and the remaining hooks spaced evenly across the width of the curtain.

- Hook a curtain hook on to each runner or ring. It helps to have someone support the bulk of the curtains while you do this.

- Finally, for a really professional finish, steam the curtains with a small hand-held steamer to help the fabric drape well.

Screws and wallplugs

Most curtaining systems come with suitable screws, and sometimes even wallplugs.

- If you are fixing to a hollow wall away from a stud position, use special expanding plugs that have flanges to grip the inside of the wall as you tighten the screw.

- Solid walls, of brick or other building blocks, have to be drilled so that you can fit plastic wallplugs to grip the screw in place.

- If you need to drill into concrete (many windows have a concrete lintel above them) use an electric drill that has a hammerhead action to make a neat hole to take the wallplug.

- Most brackets are easier screwed into wood than directly into a wall. Often, the solution is to fit a wooden batten to the wall above the window – particularly if the walls are timber-framed, or the plasterwork is uneven. Use a batten of 12 × 50mm (½ × 2in) planed (PAR, planed all round) softwood, which is 5cm (2in) shorter than the track or pole so that it will be hidden behind the curtain heading.

Facts and figures

WORK IN EITHER imperial or metric, but do not mix the measurements. For quick reference, a series of conversion charts is given below: detailed conversions of small amounts, fabric yardage/metrage and common fabric widths. These last two charts are for use in stores that sell by the metre when you have worked out quantities in yards.

Fabric lengths

1/8yd	=	10cm
1/4yd	=	20cm
3/8yd	=	40cm
1/2yd	=	45cm
5/8yd	=	60cm
3/4yd	=	70cm
7/8yd	=	80cm
1yd	=	1m
1 1/2yd	=	1.4m
2yd	=	1.9m
2 1/4yd	=	2m
2 1/2yd	=	2.3m
2 3/4yd	=	2.5m
3yd	=	2.7m
3 1/4yd	=	3m
3 1/2yd	=	3.2m
3 3/4yd	=	3.5m
4yd	=	3.7m
4 3/8yd	=	4m
4 1/2yd	=	4.2m
4 7/8yd	=	4.5m
5yd	=	4.6m
5 1/2yd	=	5m
10yd	=	9.2m
10 7/8yd	=	10m
20yd	=	18.5m
21 1/3yd	=	20m

Fabric widths

36in	=	90cm
44/45in	=	115cm
48in	=	120cm
60in	=	150cm

1in = 2.54cm
(2.5cm approx)

1cm = 0.3937in
(3/8in approx)

1ft = 0.3048m

3ft = 1yd = 1m (approx)

1m = 3.281ft

Glossary

Acrylic Synthetic fibre used to make fabric that has similar properties to wool.

Appliqué Method of decorating fabric by stitching on shapes cut from other fabrics.

Austrian blind Elaborate blind made like a curtain, with the addition of rings and cords on the back so that the panel can be pulled up during the day.

Basket weave Woven effect in fabric with several strands of warp and weft threads running together to create a small block effect.

Batten Strip of wood: fine battens are fitted into casings at the bottom of Roman blinds and roller blinds, to keep the fabric taut; more substantial battens are fixed to walls above windows to provide an even surface for curtain tracks.

Binding (bias and straight cut) Narrow strips of fabric used to cover the edge of a larger panel of fabric; bias binding is cut diagonally across the fabric (on the bias) so that it can be eased around curves without pleats and puckers.

Bouclé Yarn spun with a loose, looped finish; fabric woven or knitted from bouclé yarn.

Bound buttonholes Tailored buttonholes finished with strips of fabric binding, rather than machine or hand buttonhole stitch.

Bradawl Small pointed tool, similar to a screwdriver, used to make holes in wooden surfaces before screwing in screws, hooks, etc.

Braid Woven trimming, used in upholstery or for topstitched decorations; braids are more substantial, and often more elaborately woven, than ribbons.

Brocade Medium- to heavyweight fabric, woven in two colours to create a satin background with a relief pattern.

Broderie anglaise Cotton fabric that has been pierced and embroidered to create a decorative effect; available both as a full-width fabric and as a narrow trim; usually white or cream in colour.

Bump Thick fabric, traditionally a loosely woven brushed cotton, which is used both to improve the wear of curtains and to give curtains and other soft furnishings a soft and luxurious feel.

Calico Medium-weight cotton cloth, usually white or unbleached

Canopy Fabric suspended over a bed or other feature in a room.

Cased heading A simple curtain heading made by stitching a casing, which is slotted on to a curtain wire, rod or pole.

Casing A channel in a piece of fabric made by folding over the top and making two lines of stitching; used to make drawstring bags, curtain headings, etc.

Check A grid pattern, usually woven but may also be printed on to fabric.

Chenille Subtly ribbed, velvety fabric, softer in texture than velvet or corduroy.

Chintz Deriving from a Hindu word, chintz was originally a printed cotton fabric, usually glazed (glossy), but the term is nowadays used to denote any glazed cotton fabric.

Clip To cut into fabric at right angles to the raw edge, or diagonally across corners, in order to prevent the distortion of curved seams and bulk in corners when an item is turned the right side out.

Complementary colours Colours that lie on opposite sides of colour wheel: red and green; blue and orange; yellow and purple.

Corduroy Heavyweight fabric with pile woven into the fabric to form narrow ribs.

Covered buttons Buttons covered with fabric; they can be made with special button forms, which are available from haberdashery departments and stores.

Tarlatan Stiffened fabric, similar in weight to muslin.

Tartan Originating in Scotland, tartan is wool fabric woven to create a checked design; each clan or family had its own particular tartan.

Template A pattern that is used when cutting repeated identical shapes, for appliqué or patchwork, the pattern is cut out in card so that it can be used over and over again.

Tenting Fabric used to cover the ceiling of a room, usually gathered up and stretched from a central point.

Tertiary colours Colours containing all of the three primary colours.

Tester Canopy over a bedhead.

Thread count The number of threads in a specified area (a square inch) of a woven fabric.

Ticking Tightly woven fabric that has a distinctive woven stripe; traditionally featherproof with black

and off-white stripes, but now available in a range of natural and muted colours.

Tie-back Decorative band which is made of fabric or length of cord or rope, used in order to hold drapes clear of a window or bedhead.

Toile de Jouy Cotton fabric, originating in 18th-century France, with figurative scenes printed in a single colour on to a neutral background.

Topstitching A bold line of stitches used to emphasize seams or finish hems.

Touch-and-close fastening Synthetic fastening, which is made of two strips with plastic loops on one half, which link into a furry pile on the other strip, which is stitched to the opposite side of an opening.

Trim To cut away excess fabric.

Tussah Silk spun from the cocoons of a particular type of silkworm that feeds on oak leaves

Twill (weave) A weave in which the warp threads form a diagonal rib over the surface of the cloth.

Valance 'Skirt' around a bed that hides the bed base and legs; gathered fabric strip across the top of a window treatment that hides tracks and poles.

Velvet Woven fabric with a pile; may be made from a wide range of fibres.

Venetian blind Manufactured blind, traditionally made with wooden slats, although modern ones may have aluminium or plastic slats; the slats may be adjusted open or closed, or the blind can be raised.

Vertical blind Manufactured blinds made up from strips of stiffened fabric, hung from a track. The strips can be adjusted to hang parallel to the window for privacy, opened out, or drawn to one side of the window.

Voile Translucent fabric used mainly for drapes. It may be made of cotton or synthetic fibre.

Wallplugs Plastic or fibre tubes (straight or tapered) that are fitted into holes drilled in walls to secure screws.

Warp The threads running up and down a woven piece of cloth.

Weft The threads running across a woven piece of cloth.

Wild silk Silk fabric made from natural silk fibre, but not from the Bombyx mori (mulberry silk worm) native to China.

Yarn Thread (natural or man-made fibre) that has been spun or twisted so that it can be woven or used for embroidery or knitting.

Primary colours The three basic colours – red, blue and yellow – from which all other colours can be mixed (with the addition of black and white).

Provençal print A small, geometric interpretation of paisley patterns, printed in strong colours on lightweight plain-weave cotton.

Pucker Unsightly gathering along a seam line, caused by a blunt needle or a bulky seam.

PVC A plastic coating applied to fabrics to make them waterproof and wipeable.

Rayon A synthetic fibre – the first to be developed – that imitates silk.

Roller blind A simple window blind consisting of a sprung roller, a sheet of stiffened fabric and a wooden batten to stiffen the lower edge.

Roman blind A fabric blind, often lined, stiffened with wooden dowels and a batten, that can be drawn by a system of cords and rings.

Ruching Gathering fabric to create a panel of luxurious folds.

Sateen Cotton fabric woven to produce a glossy effect on the right side.

Satin A type of weave in which warp threads run over the surface of the fabric in order to give a glossy finish; thus a silk fabric with a satin weave.

Satin stitch Closely worked stitch; may be worked in lines by sewing machine or over larger areas by hand. Used decoratively in embroidery.

Screw-eye Metal loop with a tail that has a screw thread to enable it to be fixed into wood fittings.

Scrim Stiff, loosely woven and lightweight linen fabric.

Seam allowance The allowance around the edge of a piece of fabric for making a seam. Always add a seam allowance to the finished dimensions before cutting out.

Seam line The marked or imaginary line around the edge of a piece of fabric marking the line of stitching when a seam is made.

Seam tape Firmly woven narrow cotton tape used to prevent seams from distorting. The seam tape is positioned along the seam line on the wrong side of the fabric, and stitched into the seam as layers of fabric are joined.

Secondary colours The three colours – purple, green and orange – obtained by mixing any two primary colours.

Seersucker Plain woven fabric, often striped or checked, in which groups of warp and/or weft threads are drawn tighter, creating rows of ruching down or across the fabric.

Selvage The woven, non-fraying edges of a length of fabric.

Serging machine See overlock machine.

Sheers Translucent fabric, such as net, voile, lace., hung at windows for privacy and/or effect

Shot silk Silk fabric woven with different colours for the warp and weft, creating a fabric that reflects different shades as it catches the light.

Silk dupion Fabric that is made from silk spun by a particular type of silkworm: two silkworms spin a double cocoon together, thus producing a double thread that can be unravelled for weaving.

Swag Length of fabric that is draped decoratively across the top of a window; often used in combination with tails.

Taffeta Plain fabric, usually silk, with a glossy, stiff finish.

Tail Length of fabric that is draped at the side of a window; tails are often combined with a swag; may require accurate tailoring for even a casual effect.

Take-up lever Lever on sewing machine that moves up and down to allow the thread to loop through the fabric as you stitch.

Interlining Soft fabric (usually bump or domette) that is caught inside curtains between the main fabric and the lining to give added weight and luxury and insulating properties.

Jacquard Fabric with colour-woven pattern, similar to brocade or damask, taking its name from the inventor of the loom on which it is woven.

Lambrequin Fabric-covered pelmet, shaped in order to frame the window. Lambrequins are more usually used with a blind rather than with curtains.

Lapped seam Seam made by overlapping the edges of the panels of fabric to be joined.

Lawn Fine plain-weave cotton fabric.

Layer To trim the seam allowances within a seam to different lengths, thus eliminating bulk.

Linen union Plain weave fabric made from a mixture of cotton and linen threads.

Lining Layer of fabric added to give improved wear; curtain lining fabric is usually a satin weave cotton fabric.

Liséré Embroidered and beribboned or elaborately woven fabrics and trims.

London blind A fabric blind, usually lined, with an arrangement of cord and two rows of rings to draw up the blind in soft scoops; similar to a Roman blind, but without the stiffening dowels.

Mercerized cotton thread Sewing thread that has been specially treated in order to improve wear and look more lustrous.

Monochromatic scheme Colour scheme that uses only one colour (plus white) in varying tones.

Monotones Scheme using only one tone of a colour.

Motif Abstract or figurative outline or pattern on printed or woven fabric, or pattern used for embroidery, appliqué etc.

Muslin Fine, loosely woven cotton fabric, usually in white or natural.

Nets Translucent curtains, hung to give privacy to windows.

Notch To cut a V-shaped wedge out of the seam allowance, so that pieces of fabric can be matched when they are being stitched together, and to reduce bulk in curved seams when an item is turned the right side out.

Organdie Fine, stiff cotton open-weave fabric, now often available in synthetic fibres.

Organza Finely woven stiff silk, made from a particular type of twisted silk yarn.

Ottoman Heavy, twill-weave fabric, in silk, cotton, linen or synthetic fibre.

Overlock sewing machine Advanced machine that forms stitches in a more elaborate way than a traditional sewing machine; particularly useful for stretch fabric.

Paisley An intricate pattern with elongated and curved oval motifs, originating in India but taking its name from the Scottish town renowned for its textile industry.

Pelmet A wooden or fabric-covered box, fixed over the heading of a curtain to cover tracks and offer protection from dust.

Pelmet shelf A wooden shelf fitted above a window; the front of the pelmet box or a valance is normally fitted to the front of the pelmet shelf.

Petersham ribbon Hard-wearing, ribbed ribbon, traditionally made of silk.

Pile The 'fur' of a carpet or of a velvety fabric.

Piqué Light- or medium-weight cotton fabric woven in a single colour with a fine, embossed effect.

Plaid Colour-woven fabric (check).

Polyester wadding Thick, soft, lightweight padding which is available in standard widths and thicknesses.

Damask Fabric (usually silk or linen) with a pattern woven into it; often woven in a single colour, so that the pattern only shows as the light catches the fabric.

Denim Originally from the city of Nîmes in France, a twill weave fabric that was traditionally woven using indigo warp and white weft threads.

Dobby weave Fabric woven with small, repeating pattern, such as a small diamond or a raised star.

Domette Soft fabric, often synthetic, used as a layer of padding in curtains or under tablecloths.

Dowel Length of rounded wood, fitted in casings to keep Roman blinds hanging crisply when they are drawn up.

Dress curtains Permanently fixed curtains that are not intended to be drawn closed. They are often used in combination with a roller or Roman blind.

Dressmaker's carbon paper Paper with coloured coating on the back, so that when you trace an outline on to it the motif is transferred to a layer of fabric placed beneath the carbon paper.

Easy-care fabrics Usually woven from a mix of fibres, and requiring minimal ironing.

Electronic sewing machine Electric sewing machine with microchips to make it easy to adjust the type, size and tension of the stitch.

Facing Panel of fabric used to back the main fabric of an item around an edge, giving a neat finish.

Faille Silk fabric with a ribbed weave.

Festoon blind Blind with a gathered heading and vertical tapes to gather the fabric into festoons. The blind is raised with a system of rings and cords.

Field The background colour of a printed or embroidered piece of fabric.

Finials Decorative knobs, loops and twirls made of wood, metal or plastic, supplied to fit on the end of curtain tracks or poles.

Flat seam A simple seam used to join two pieces of fabric with a single line of stitching.

French seam Double seam in which the raw edges are completely enclosed.

Geometric print Regular print, of abstract shapes arranged in a regular pattern.

Gingham Lightweight woven fabric, usually white and one other colour, originally a striped fabric, but now used to describe check.

Grain of fabric The lengthways grain is the direction in which the warp threads of the fabric run, parallel to the selvages.

Ground The 'background' fabric used in embroidery, appliqué etc.

Heading tape A specially manufactured tape that is stitched across the top of a curtain; it has an arrangement of cords so that the curtain can be gathered and gaps for curtain hooks to be slotted through the tape.

Herringbone A fine, hand-sewn stitch that is used to join panels of wadding or to hold hems in place; may also be used decoratively as an embroidery stitch.

Hold-back Metal or wooden knob or hook, which is fitted, usually to either side of a window, so that the curtains can be looped and draped clear of the window.

Ikat Fabric woven from predyed yarn; the yarn is coloured in sections so that predyed patches are woven in next to each other in order to create a pattern.

Interfacing Layer of fabric, often synthetic, non-woven and iron-on, which is used in order to stiffen lightweight fabrics and make them easier to handle. In soft furnishings it may be used to stiffen curtain headings or fabrics to be used for appliqué motifs.

Index

Acknowledgements

Photography

Anna French 32, 46

Laura Ashley Home Autumn/Winter 2000
Collection 5 bottom, 10

Harlequin 6, 36, 43, 52, 58, 60 bottom

Next Home Autumn/Winter 2000 Collection 24, 53
top

Ocotpus Publishing Ltd.

    Nadia Bryant back cover top, 8 bottom,

    Paul Forrester 20 bottom, 56 top

    Rupert Horrox 4 top, 11, 13 top, 14 top, 14
    bottom, 18, 30 top, 30 bottom, 39, 59

    Di Lewis 1 bottom, 55

    David Loftus 9 bottom

    Peter Myers 1 top, 7, 23

    David Parmitter front cover bottom, back cover
    Centre, 8 top, 12, 15, 19, 20 top, 21 bottom, 22,
    26, 27, 31, 35, 41, 45 top, 45 bottom, 50, 51 top,
    51 bottom, 54

    Paul Ryan back cover bottom, 38, 48

    John Sims 9 top

    Debi Treloar 5 top, 5 bottom, 21 top, 29, 60 top,
    61, 62, 69

    Polly Wreford 28

Osborne & Little Plc 3, 49, 53 bottom

Parker Hobart Associates 13 bottom

Sanderson 25, 34, 44, 56 bottom

Elizabeth Whiting & Associates front cover top, 2

For Hamlyn

Editorial Manager: Jane Birch

Senior Designer: Claire Harvey

Project Manager: Jo Lethaby

Designer: Mark Stevens

Picture Researcher: Christine Junemann

Senior Production Controller: Louise Hall

Illustrator: Jane Hughes